THE DOUBT DEMOLISHER

THE 10 "BEs" to BEING A BETTER YOU

ANTHONY BROUGHTON

INSPIRATIONAL VOYAGES WITH MISTER, LLC

For bulk orders, speaking engagements, workshops, or educational
consulting, contact us at **www.misterbinspires.com**

ISBN: 978-0-578-62958-2

ANTHONY BROUGHTON

THE DOUBT DEMOLISHER

CONTENTS

DEDICATION

To my mother Vera Broughton: Thank you for inspiring me to always go above and beyond in all that I do. When I wanted to give up, you pushed me to DEMOLISH DOUBT! To my father James "Anthony" Broughton: Thank you for your guidance, advice, and always instilling in me a robust work ethic. To my step mother, Deloris Broughton: Thank you for always loving and supporting me unconditionally. My sisters Anastashia, Shakaisha, Shiquita, and Dakota, inspire me BEyond their imaginations! I strive to BE better every day to make you proud and to BE an effective role-model. I love you, strong, Black, resilient, and intelligent queens! Continue to raise the bar. Blaze your trail of excellence for others!

Honoring the Elders

I've learned to value and appreciate the presence and the legacy of elders. I could not begin writing this book without honoring the elders and my ancestors! I would BE remiss if I pursued the process of BEing a better me without seeking the counsel of the elders. I pause to honor some of my elders: Mildred Wigfall Green (Don't allow anyone to stop you from achieving your goals), Mildred Broughton (Always show and demand respect. Keep God first), James Broughton (Work hard and take pride in your work. Always BE willing to share your gift with others), Rosa Lee Pinckney ("Take care of yourself"), Caldwell Pinckney, Sr. (Work hard to ensure your business positively impacts the community), Charlie Wigfall, Sr. (Cherish family time), Lily Wigfall (Stand with grace and pride), and Rebecca Broughton Smith (Live life to the fullest). I am BETTER because **I chose to apply their wisdom.**

Acknowledgments

God
The Wigfall, Nelson, Pinckney, Broughton, & Singleton families
Jerusalem United Methodist Church & The Cross, SC Community
The "highly acclaimed" Call Me MISTER Program
Benedict College, my alma mater
Alpha Phi Alpha Fraternity, Incorporated (Special love to the SC chapters and the Alpha Psi Lambda chapter)
The Claflin University Family & Dr. Dwaun J. Warmack
Claflin University School of Education
Orangeburg County First Steps
Brookland Baptist Church

To the person who doubted their abilities.
To the person who doubted their gift.
To the person who doubted their potential.
To the person who doubted they'd ever amount to anything.
To the person who doubted their worth.
To the person who doubted their ability to pass a standardized test.
To the person who doubted their ability to achieve their certificate, diploma, or degree.
To the person who doubted their purpose.
To the person who doubted they would make it this far.
You will demolish doubt.

Introduction

INTRODUCTION

To BE or to BEcome?

Many of us desire to BE better. We desire to have better lives, be better family members, better lovers, better friends, better employees, better owners, better leaders, and simply better people. To some, better means more advanced or more refined. To many, it means a personal upgrade. To others, BEing better means engaging in self-improvement. To me, BEing better means all of the above, with the addition of relentlessly BEing happier and holistically healthier, as you elevate your BEing towards BEcoming.

Unfortunately, many of us envision our better selves as someone we will evolve into—which is true. We begin generating visions of our future selves. We envision ourselves opening the door to our new store, BEing promoted to a new position, or relishing a happy relationship. Many of us take it a step further in late December, when we create New Year resolutions in hopes of transforming into a "new me" when the clock strikes twelve. Snap out of it! Snap-Snap! If we are not careful we will live vicariously through the future. There is so much work for us to do in this very moment. Although we should envision who and what we desire to become, we should not stifle ourselves by focusing solely on something that has yet to exist. Faith without works is dead, but more importantly, tomorrow isn't promised. Yes, we should honor and respect the process of BEcoming, but what about NOW?

What about our responsibility to operate in the present? What about our capacity to simply BE? We should not take that for granted. Live in the now!

What I've learned is that BEing and BEcoming are choices. If we desire to change, we must be *willing* to make the conscious choice to change—right now! You don't have to wait until next year or tomorrow to BE better; you can BE better right now! By BEing who you are in pursuit of BEcoming, you have the power to commit to making the necessary changes in the present moment. You may not have the Benz you wished for, but you can begin BEing who you need to BE and doing what you need to do, *right now* to get the Benz. If you want to BEcome a doctor, start thinking, studying, paying attention and helping like a doctor, right now! You don't have to wait! The doctor is already within you, awaiting for you to do the work to develop the doctor within! You can BE the doctor right now, but you will BECOME licensed through your journey. So yes, respect the process. Yes, prepare for the future, but never underestimate the power of NOW! You don't just go out and BEcome who and what you desire. You must search within and then call forth that doctor, lawyer, teacher—essentially, your best self to rise up from within.

To BEcome, you must first master the art of BEing! If you can't BE who you are, you will BEcome someone else! It's a choice! The rationale for focusing on BEing is bitter-sweet, but straightforward: You are human, and life is short. Therefore, we must do what I underscore in Chapter 1, which is to BE Grateful.

BEing BETTER is not *just* about YOU. We learn through messages in society about our roles and responsibilities as individuals. One of the most prominent messages I subscribed to was the idea I must strive for achievement! I must win! I must BE on top! I must lead! I must BE the best I can BE. I must BE the 'American' Dream— whatever that means. I-I-I-I-I-I! Although much of society tends to focus on competition and individualism, which is deeply rooted in Western societies, this book embraces collectivism (inspired by the West African concept of communalism). Contrary to popular belief, your process of BEing a BETTER you is not an isolated process. You are not alone! The development of others is inextricably connected to your evolution. BEing a BETTER you is connected to a BETTER community and a BETTER world. To be clear, you only get to define BETTER from your reality, not others. In the words of Dr. Christopher Emdin, "the only person BETTER than you is embedded in you."

In Chapter 5: BE Studious, we will explore ways people and experiences play an integral role as "teachers" during our journey to BEing as we are BEcoming. You will learn that even when you feel lonely, there are both teachers and educators along the way to support you in your journey. Suppose you fail to BE open-minded, which is examined in Chapter 3. In that case, you will increase the likelihood of experiencing metaphorically closed and locked doors, roadblocks, burned bridges, prison, and self-sabotage. Your commitment to BEing BETTER will inspire others to BE better. Therefore, although it is easy and possibly selfish to perceive your process of BEing as an isolated venture, Chapter 4: BE Accountable will support you in considering your responsibilities to others during your journey. The power to BE is already invested within you, if you work consistently to develop within! In Chapter 7: BE Consistent, you will explore the power of BEing consistent with sculping and BEing sculpted by your experiences. Life presents us with priceless opportunities to learn, grow, and BE enlightened by the teachable moments embedded within our experiences. However, if we do not take care of ourselves during the process, as explored in Chapter 6: BE Self-caring, we will not grow to our fullest potential and compromise our lives.

We must continuously learn how to BE Impactful (Chapter 8). To do this, we must do the work of overcoming doubt! Through reflection, I've learned that overcoming doubt was an integral part of my process. Each big and small milestone came with the company of doubters, both internally and externally. I chose to face the beast of the sea. I decided to meet the raging waters. I decided to step out on faith. I decided to trust my creator, who can and has calmed calamity. I chose to anchor my soul in things that are eternal! I decided to face fear and to demolish doubt. I decided to speak back to the voices in my head that said I couldn't, shouldn't, and wouldn't BE Extraordinary (Chapter 9) by pushing myself to manifest what I should and could with the power invested in me. I chose to be a DOUBT DEMOLISHER! As examined in Chapter 7: BE P.E.T.T.Y., you have to purposefully entertain those things you desire to BE (Chapter 10) in your pursuit of BEcoming.

This book is designed for you to use in meaningful ways as you grow through what you go through. Although I share recommendations and "teachable moments" throughout this book, I want to affirm that your truths and realities also matter, so "right" or "wrong" answers or perspectives are truthfully determined through your lens. BEing a BETTER you is a self-discovery process amid a continuum of re-self-discovery as we co-discover ourselves with others. Yes, many may perceive this as an individual journey, but you are not alone. Feel free to exchange thoughts and ideas regarding concepts explored in this book with others. This book isn't intended to provide you with 'the' ways to BE a BETTER you. So, abstain from using a one-size-fits-all approach when reading this book. I chose to share my methods of BEing to inspire others to focus on BEing BETTER as they BEcome better. Dr. Maya Angelou said, "When you get, give. When you learn, teach." This concept inspired me to give and teach what I've learned! Thus, I share with you the mindset that shaped what I now refer to as the Doubt Demolisher, in hopes of inspiring you to demolish doubt to BE who you've been called to BE.

Doubt

Doubt <u>can</u> BE a disorder. It <u>can</u> be an impairment to your full potential. Doubt <u>can</u> disrupt your ability to thrive. It will paralyze you <u>if you allow it</u>. The consistent, repetitive, and overwhelming negative thoughts and deficit perspectives can constrain your upward mobility. Doubt will have you questioning if you are worthy to live. It can also trigger the imposter syndrome. You may doubt yourself even when others strongly believe in you. Doubt is so difficult to demolish or overcome because all of what and how we believe is influenced by our socialization. The messages we received about ourselves through our interactions in society and with family and friends, as we acquire values, beliefs, attitudes, customs, and practices, shape how and what we think. Mass Media also has a major influence on how and what we think and believe. Television shows, social media, radio, music, videos, movies, and images all shape our minds and influences our behavior.

The Doubt Demolisher Challenge #1

Only listen to or watch positive, uplifting, and inspirational podcasts, songs, videos, movies, and television shows for one week. Create a playlist of inspirational and uplifting music from various genres. Do not limit yourself to one genre. Watch inspirational TED talks or motivational messages on YouTube. Subscribe to podcasts that are uplifting and inspirational. Try this for a week and you should notice a change in your thoughts, emotions, and behavior. Much of how we feel, think, and act is influenced by what we consume! Doubt is a symptom of toxic consumption. Similar to your body, you will not BE better until you release the toxins that are causing dis-ease.

Some of us have unknowingly learned, embraced, and engaged in toxic and destructive social and self-patterns. Self-doubt thereby becomes our default mindset, harboring and replaying the negative thoughts, statements, and images from our lived experiences. Self-doubt is a symptom of internalizing the oppressive, destructive, and dehumanizing noise of the *world*. Many of us are still dealing with some of the past. The comment that someone made in middle school about you being "too big" to do gymnastics may still BE impacting you.

However, you must remember to, "Never measure your worth using another person's ruler!" -Unknown. Although doubt is closely related to fear, fear can be beneficial. Healthy fear is linked to our common sense. You can say, "I do not fear tigers! I will go attack it," but you will be demolished if the tiger isn't trained. You can say, "I do not fear diving off a boat in the middle of the ocean, but if you cannot swim, you will drown. Healthy fear is tied to our physical safety. So, whatever you do, never lose your common sense.

Bogged Down in Self-Doubt

Yes, doubt can paralyze you. It's like being bogged down in mud. Regardless of hard you press the gas or how positive you are, the car will remain bogged down in the mud. You need help! You need to be pulled from out of the mud. It's ok to ask for help! Throughout this book, I will unleash approaches that could help you overcome doubt. Throughout my life, elders have always provided me with the wisdom I needed to pull myself out of the muddy waters of life. Therefore, I begin this book by honoring the elders.

Honoring the Elders

I do not speak or make any movements without honoring the elders, my ancestors, and the Great IAM that dwelled and continues to live through them.

I don't seek the counsel of elders only when I need something. I appreciate BEing in their physical presence as well. Elders are so profoundly robust that their words and works radiate a vibrancy of passion and excellence long after they've ascended beyond the physical realm. Their BEing transcends generations. I'm still encouraged by the words of my grandmother, great grandparents, great grand aunts/uncles, W.E.B DuBois, Maya Angelou, Carter G. Woodson, Benjamin E. Mayes, James Baldwin, Fannie Lou Hamer, Toni Morrison, Cicely Tyson, Asa Hilliard, and Frantz Fanon—amongst many others! Thus, I'm grateful for their existence, legacy, and BEing. It is because of their BEing that I can BE—UBUNTU. I am because they are! In West African culture, griots are highly revered advisors who pass down oral traditions through story-telling. They are living libraries with experiential knowledge. I have gained so much insight from elders because **I was willing to listen to them.** Oftentimes, we tend to speak confidently about what we *think* we know upon earning our advanced degrees. However, a moment with the elders will awaken you to distinguish between knowledge and wisdom. I learned that knowledge is simply knowing, and wisdom is having discernment based on a deep understanding of the lessons life has taught us. Knowledge tells you that it is raining outside. Wisdom tells you that you should not stand in the rain for extended periods because you could get sick. The knowledge of the elders has never failed me. **You have to BE and remain teachable! "It's hard to hear God's voice when you've already determined what you want Him to say."**

Elders will unapologetically remind you of who you are through love, as they keep you grounded with wisdom. We must love and respect them for who they were, who they are, and who they will 'BEcome' as they continue to BE. Remember, a wise man/woman is slow to speak! So, when we are amongst these legends, we should listen and BE in the moment –not on our cell phones. So, I pause to allow one of my elders to enlighten you with words of wisdom regarding the power of BEing. I present to you, Queen Mother Mrs. Julia Richardson-Wright.

THE POWER OF BEING

The wisdom of Mrs. Julia Richardson-Wright

IMITATION of another is like committing suicide! When one discovers who one IS, not WAS, then one has the potential of Being who one is created to BE. Jesus, the Christ said, before Abraham was, I AM. The power of the verb to BE begins with I AM. We are Spirit Being in human clothing. Out of 8 billion people in the Universe, you are the only one with your fingerprints, which stands to reason that you are to unequivocally BE. BE imperfect and allow perfection to flow: BE ordinary and see the Extraordinary; BE common and observe the Uncommon; BE simple and allow the Profound. BE curious! BE vulnerable! BE risky! BE gut-level honest with self. BE willing to uncover and discover! BE fully present! BE open! The power of BEing is just to BE! And No one, absolutely no one, can tell you how to BE. One cannot practice Being because being is just who you are! You are naturally spiritual and spiritually natural. When BEing flows, IMITATION goes! The power of BEing is magical! Work IT!

[Internal Truth].

"Seeing yourself, knowing yourself, and speaking truth to yourself is freeing. Sometimes we are full of what others told us about who we are as oppose to us knowing who we are according to our Creator. To thine own self speak truth!"

CHAPTER 1

BE GRATEFUL

BE GRATEFUL

"Having an attitude of gratitude will increase your altitude."
-Anthony Broughton

Affirmation: I will overcome doubting my purpose. I am grateful for life. I am grateful for who I am and who I shall become.

If you are reading this, BE grateful for life, sight, and the ability to read these words. We often take simple privileges for granted. The stark reality is that each of those privileges can BE taken away at any given moment. We often think about what we're going to do when we get home or this weekend. We also begin thinking about a thrilling vacation we're going to take at the end of the month. We make our plans in advance, *knowing* that we will have an awesome time when the time comes. The hard reality is that tomorrow isn't promised. In fact, the next minute or hour isn't promised. We must relish the present moment for our current ability to BE—to not just exist, but to also live. That fender bender could've been a fatal car accident. That surgery could've gone wrong. That earthquake could've destroyed your house. That pandemic could've destroyed you. That depression could've taken you out, BUT you are *still* here! What could've and should've taken you out didn't, so you have a reason to BE grateful!

You should've been six feet under, but you're six feet over!

The fact that you are alive is an indication that there is more work for you to do. The mere fact that you beat approximately 1.2 billion sperm cells to the egg means you were born a winner. You were born with a purpose. You've been chosen to fulfill a purpose here on Earth. You will discover your purpose in your pursuit of BEing as you BEcome. You are a winner. Remember who you are!

Know and Remember Your Who

People say that you should know your why? Typically, they are referring to knowing your purpose, or knowing why you do what you do. Although it is essential for you to know your why, you must first **know and remember your who**. You must know who you are and whose you are. So, who are you? Typically, when asked, people respond with their name. However, you are not your name. Your name is what you are called, not who you are. This is oftentimes so difficult to answer because we have been so accustomed to responding with our name, but a name is just a small part of our identity. So again, who are you?

Our identity as spirits having natural experiences in this physical realm is multidimensional and intersectional. We are an amalgamation of BEings. In fact, a mantra that has fueled my passion to BE BETTER each day is a quote by Dr. Maya Angelou, "I come as one, but I stand as 10,000." I am reminded that I am not alone! When I stand, I stand proudly on the shoulders of my ancestors. I stand on solid rock with a badge of honor and a crown that has been paid for by the blood, sweat, and tears of my ancestors. They fought, died, and were murdered in pursuit of freedom. I AM because they were! I am because we are

(Ubuntu). Ubuntu is a South African concept that means *togetherness*. My greatness is a result of those who have paved the way for me to BE great! Who am I not to BE great?

It's because of the activism of my ancestors that I was able to write this book. Life has taught me that knowing and remembering who you are and from whence you came plays an essential role in BEcoming a BEtter you. You didn't BEcome who you are in isolation. Yes, your current success is a result of your hard work, but it is also because of the sacrifices and the provisions those before you made, so you'd have the privilege of BEing where you are today. Some of us wouldn't survive a day in our ancestors' shoes.

I use enslaved Africans rather than calling my ancestors slaves because they shouldn't BE reduced to a term that defines the conditions they were forced into, even though they rebelled. They were African kings and queens who were so intelligent and intentional they planted seeds in their crowns (hair) so they would BE prepared to grow crops wherever they ended up. Dr. Adelaide Sanford, an elder, taught me that. They were prepared during the most humiliating circumstances, yet some of us can't even remember to bring essential items from home to successfully perform tasks at work or school on the regular. I am grateful for who they were because they inspire me to live each day of my life to the fullest, to honor their strength, bravery, resilience, intellect, innovation, passion, talents, resourcefulness, boldness and wit. If I ever lose my sense of purpose or wonder why am I here, I can always think back at what my ancestors endured and BE reminded that "I am the dream and the hope of the [en]slave[d]," as Dr. Maya Angelou once proclaimed. My purpose then becomes to BE their dream and to manifest their hopes through how **I choose** to live my life. As a result,

"I stand not only as 10,000

but as 10,000 to the tenth power!"

-Oprah Winfrey

It Could BE Worse, BUT I'm *Still* Here

"I'm poor, Black, I might even BE ugly, but dear God, I'm here. I'm here."
-The Color Purple Movie

I am reminded by Celie Harris Johnson in the movie *The Color Purple* that although we may BE a lot of things, we should be BE grateful to BE here. I might BE ugly to you, but I'm here. I might not BE where I want to BE, but I'm here. I might not have money in my pocket, but I'm here. That alone is priceless. When you disconnect and rise above dead situations, you can appreciate the smallest yet the biggest things in life. You can celebrate the pulse on your wrist because you survived or know someone who survived a near-death experience.

When I am depressed and it feels like things aren't working out, I've learned to begin counting my blessings, naming them one by one. I begin to remember that:

I heard my alarm sound off this morning. *Someone wasn't able to hear it.* I woke up this morning. *Some people didn't.* I woke up in my own bed. *Many people woke up in the hospital.* I can remember my name. *Some people woke up and did not know their name due to Alzheimer's.* I can feel my hands and feet. *Some people are unable to feel their extremities.* *Some people do not have hands or feet.* I still have a roof over my head.

There are many people who are homeless. I have food to eat and water drink. *There are people who are starving across the globe.* I have earned a high school diploma. *There are many people who dropped out of high school and have not **yet** completed it.*

The list goes on and on. While we could easily focus on what's going wrong, we must BE grateful for what's going right! In fact, I've learned that everything that's going wrong could BE going worse. Sometimes the very thing that we think is going wrong is in the process of working out for our good.

> "One day you will look back at that closed door and laugh at how small-minded you were. Sometimes there's nothing behind that door for YOU. "
>
> -Anthony Broughton

Anthony Broughton
June 1, 2016 ·

MiSTER Dr. B is transparently reflective this morning to inspire someone. He says, "Yep, that position I applied for and knew I was qualified over the person who was selected with no early childhood credentials or classroom experience. It tore me up internally because I was passionate and loyal to my job . Created an entire vision for the school for someone else to manifest (epic fail) Meanwhile he didn't last long....But when I tell you that denial has put me on a whole different level with increased pay, benefits, resources, and leadership position! I can't even consider going back to where I used to be! The unjust doesn't prosper! Don't cry about those closed doors, thank God for them!!! Praising God that I'm not concerned or worried about that door 😊 ▮▮▮▮▮▮▮▮▮▮▮▮▮▮▮" No apologies needed 😊👊

My mother once told me, "The unjust won't prosper." That closed door that I once cried about is now for sale. Yes, the entire building is for sale. Sometimes we think we know what's best for ourselves, but life has a unique way of reminding us that we are not in control of everything. Sometimes demons disguised as people with hidden agendas who may not align with our purpose maybe on the other side of the door! Sometimes closed doors may BE divine intervention to prevent us from opening doors to places that would suffocate our gifts. Of course, enduring the pain and suffering can BE extremely rough in the moment. Rejection isn't easy to deal with. In fact, rejection is God's protection.

I look at where I am now and thank God for the closed doors that led me to a place that supports me in manifesting my gifts and talents to positively impact others. Sometimes we **doubt** ourselves, questioning whether or not we are good enough for the job, or whether or not we are qualified. We **doubt** our potential, questioning why we would even consider such a job. Sometimes we begin to question our purpose after countless hours of listening to those negative voices in our heads. However, somehow, someway we always hear a message from someone or something that reminds us that (in the words of the old folk), "Everything is gone' BE alright!"

It is custom for Christians to project onto you Psalms 30:5, "…weeping may endure for a night, but joy cometh in the morning" in hopes of encouraging you during your dark moments. I must admit, sometimes it seems as though words are insufficient. I need my troubles to BE over when I wake up. I could never find joy in the morning, until something forced me to change my perspective. One morning I woke up to a call that began with, "Have you heard what happened to your cousin?" At that moment my heart sank, but I began to realize that joy was the privilege of seeing another day in spite of my trials and tribulations. We may BE grieving. We may BE sad. We may BE experiencing drama at work or in our homes, but we are yet *still* alive. BE grateful!

We have so many reasons to BE grateful. Someone is praying for the blessing you're taking for granted. You complained about your neighbors playing their music so loudly in the apartment next door, but at least you didn't have to hear it sleeping on the streets. You're complaining about your job, but at least you have one. No matter how bad you think your life is or how bad you think your circumstances are, it could BE worse. Someone took the same cards you've been dealt and played them in ways that yielded positive results. How are you playing your cards? I've seen a highly skilled violinist play her violin with a prosthetic arm. **What's your excuse?** I know of students who didn't have electricity, but they completed their assignments under candlelight. **What's your excuse?** I know of people who did not have access to Wi-Fi to complete a project at home, so they drove to a restaurant to complete the task. **What's your excuse?** I've seen a person with no limbs drive a car and accomplish daily tasks without assistance. **What's your excuse?**

BEing ungrateful will teach you quickly to appreciate what you have. Take the gift that you have and work it! That's exactly what I have done. I took my gift of music, art, teaching, and speaking and I worked it. My mother ensured I always had writing and drawing utensils everywhere I went. She didn't have to do it, but she did. BE grateful for the people in your life who helped you get to where you are. The time you spend on focusing on what you don't have, you can spend BEing grateful for what you do have.

The same energy you apply towards focusing on what you don't have is the same energy you need to apply towards putting

in the work to acquire what you desire. You may not like who you are right now, but there's someone wishing to BE you! Believe it or not, there is someone who wishes they were in your shoes. In fact, while we are wishing for another pair of sneakers, there is someone without that privilege.

- **Person 1:** I want another pair of Jordans.

- **Person 2:** I want Jordans.

- **Person 3:** I want name-brand sneakers.

- **Person 4:** I want sneakers.

- **Person 5:** I want a shoe.

- **Person 6:** I want socks.

- **Person 7:** I want feet.

That was an example of seven different people with seven different realities. Person 7 wishes they had feet, while Person 1 is wishing they possessed another pair of Jordans. BE grateful for what you have. People say the grass is greener on the other side, but the grass isn't greener on the other side. The grass is greener wherever you water and fertilize it. Sometimes we worry about if the grass is greener on the other side, but we haven't even planted grass seeds in our own yard. Worry about your stuff! On the other hand, while we are wishing our grass is greener like the other side, it is actually turf. Things aren't always what they appear to BE. Some people pray for blessings and don't even yet have the capacity to receive it. You desire a king size bed but you have a twin size room. You want a house on the hill, but you don't even have land on the hill. In the words of my geechie people, "Ee eye longa dan ee mout" (Their eyes are longer than their mouth). Simply put, don't bite off more than you can chew. Your gratefulness will open the door to more things to be grateful for. BE GRATEFUL.

"Thank you"

If you are truly thankful for what and who you have in your life, you should commit to living gratefully. You should demonstrate thanksgiving daily. To BE thankful is to verbally express gratitude for a kind gesture rendered. When someone gives you a gift, you respond with an expression of gratitude by saying, "thank you." However, when you are grateful for the gift you received, you respond by saying "thank you," and showing gratitude through your actions. BEing grateful sometimes encompasses going beyond speaking about gratitude towards demonstrating and embodying gratitude through our daily actions. Our service is the rent we pay for living on this Earth. Let your actions speak gratitude for the life you've been given. If you appreciate someone, show them! Don't just speak it—BE it!

CHAPTER 2

BE OPEN-MINDED

BE OPEN-MINDED

"You think you know so much. Let me teach you."
Sincerely,

Life

-Anthony Broughton

Affirmation: I will overcome doubting the outcome of trying something different.

L ife has so much to offer, but our worldviews, biases, beliefs, customs, religions, and practices can limit us from BEing better. Much of who we are and how we behave is influenced by how we were socialized. We learned implicitly and explicitly which behaviors, clothing, and conversations were "appropriate" for certain settings. We also learned that our language holds power depending upon when we use it, how we use it, and with whom we use it. For instance, I would never greet my teacher with, "Aye yo, wazup bruh?" the same way I'd greet my friend. It's just something I learned.

We can limit our potential and marginalize opportunities to grow if we become confined to our norms. We shouldn't think inside the "box." In fact, we have to shatter the concept of the "box" we've often believed in we must dance beyond our comfort zone. There is no "box!" Just because you learned something doesn't make it right. Just because it's true to you doesn't mean it's everyone's truth. We can gain insight by exploring concepts from various perspectives, even if they make us uncomfortable. I hated and still hate BEing uncomfortable. I noticed that when I allowed fear to win, I built up psychological walls that mentally resisted any experiences beyond my comfort zone. We cannot afford to play with your potential. Take advantage of opportunities to expand your horizons, even when it feels uncomfortable. Growth is not a comfortable process. Fitness has taught me that the uncomfortable pain we experience during pre and post workouts is the process of gaining and expanding our muscles. Similarly, we must commit to BEing comfortable with BEing uncomfortable, so we can expand the muscles of our minds. It is in these moments that we grow stronger as we evolve, if we are truly willing to BE open-minded.

Different Isn't Deficit

Just because something is different doesn't make it a deficit. Something may not 'fit' into your norms, realities, or beliefs, but that doesn't make it deficit. What's deemed right or wrong is your truth. The whole notion of different as deficit is at the root of racism. We've got to BE way better than that. Christians are taught that there is only one God. They do not entertain the teachings of other gods like Buddha or Confucius. However, there is much we can learn from other cultures, religions, and belief systems. In fact, we would be blown away if we truly unpacked and dismantled some of our religious beliefs and the sources from which they derive. Do you truly know the origins of your religious affiliations? Do you know the history of your denomination? We have to know what we believe and why we believe it.

We all have the right to appreciate different views without subscribing to them. Exploring other perspectives, values, customs, and belief elevated and expanded my capacity to BE better. It broadened my horizons and extended my thinking. I sought to understand, rather than seeking to critique. Sometimes we get so caught up in teaching others about our beliefs that we aren't receptive to hear the beliefs of others. There is so much we can learn if we listen to learn rather than to respond. The Buddha said, "Faith and prayer are both invisible, but they make impossible things possible." He also said, "What you think, you become. What you feel, you attract. What you imagine, you create." Can we learn from these quotes? Yes! Do we have to practice Buddhism to appreciate these teachings? No. Being closed-minded marginalizes who we can BEcome, because familiarity can make us complacent. How would we grow and learn from one another if everyone thought and acted in the same manner? I had an encounter with an atheist that really pushed me to engage in deep reflection. Sometimes we need to BE challenged by a different perspective to BEcome better.

I spoke with an atheist who asked, "How is it that you have 8 churches on the same street and there are still homeless people? How is it that your religion is dominated by hypocrites? Some of the same preachers who preach against homosexuality are the same ones committing adultery. I thought no sin is greater than the other?" Why are there missing books of the Bible? Why aren't they a part of the Bible? Who got to decide? Have you studied King James? Why are some of the Bible Stories so similar to Kemetic Stories? Whoa! He challenged me non-stop. It's very difficult for people to critique or be critiqued on the things they are deeply invested in. It took me several days to digest his questions. His questions really made me reflect. The atheist inspired me to really consider how we must BE accountable for our actions. We have work to do! I listened to his perspectives and appreciated his rationales. Do I embrace them all? No. Can I appreciate them? Yes. Do I need more time to work through and reflect on them? Yes. Differences make us better. We need to BE ok with listening to people who may not hold the same beliefs we do.

We must also remember that every statement isn't always an attack. We can limit opportunities to grow if we always go into defense mode rather than in reception mode.

BEing open-minded involves BEing receptive to an eclectic array of perspectives, viewpoints, information, and ideas. It enhances our ability to think critically, deeply, and rationally. As a result, we are better prepared to make informed decisions. When we aren't open-minded, it is more challenging for us to BE empathetic. We tend to find it more challenging to consider what it's like to BE in someone else's shoes. I must admit, BEing open-minded is no easy feat. We have to bite the bullet, swallow our pride, and open our hearts and minds to learn. I always ask the following questions after listening to the ideas of others:

- Tell me more about that?
- Give me an example.
- What made you say that?
- How did you come to that point?

I usually say, "I see where you're coming from," to affirm their perspective even if I do not agree with them. When I agree to disagree, it is only after I've asked questions to really glean an understanding of how they've gotten to their perspective. It is extremely hard not to interrupt people when they have contrasting views. However, speaking to people with contrasting viewpoints can yield opportunities for others to learn from your perspective as well. You may get upset. You may be pissed, but control yourself. I've learned to bite my tongue as a commitment to sharing the conversation "space." You have to allow people an opportunity to speak without interrupting them! Remember, BEing uncomfortable is a necessary part of the growth process. Trust yourself during this process.

Jump Out of the Bowl

Being open-minded can help us expand our experiences. Many of us expect something different, yet we are in the same place doing the same things, thinking the same thoughts, in the same ways! If you want different, you have to do something different.

If you want to experience a shift,
you have to shift your thinking!

You have to shift your beliefs! You have to shift your expectations! You have to shift the gear and move! You have to make the choice that change is necessary. People who want change and don't experience it, don't want it bad enough. You have to be willing to do what is necessary to upgrade yourself. The power to shift your situation is in your hands, mind, and mouth! Some of us expect to produce a PowerPoint, but we are using a typewriter. Your advancement to the next level requires that you advance your thinking. You cannot advance yourself with antiquated and ineffective systems, approaches, and thought patterns.

Being open-minded reminds me of a gold-fish that decided to catapult from the fish bowl into the ocean. There is so much depth we can experience if we leap out on faith and into unchartered territories. The goldfish has to learn versatility to adapt to the conditions of the ocean which significantly varied from a fresh water fish bowl. The goldfish now has access to a wealth of opportunities (including life threatening ones) with sharks, sea turtles, seahorse, starfish, dolphins, and a host of tropical fishes with whom it would not have encountered in the bowl. So, we have to jump! Yes, we have to take risks. Get out and try new things. Visit a restaurant that is out of your ballpark. Attend a conference that will challenge you to grow. Engage in conversations with people in settings you wouldn't normally engage in. Read a book or a magazine in a subject area that you wouldn't typically read. Travel abroad or to different states and try different restaurants. Ask many questions while you're visiting. Sometimes we have to push ourselves to jump. In other instances the impetus to jump is ignited by our experiences or other people. This is why you have to surround yourself with people who believe in you.

Don't Hate. Invest in Yourself

When I arrived to Benedict College as number 9 in my high school graduating class, I thought I was the sharpest kid on the block.

I was so accustomed to being a big fish in a little bowl. I quickly learned there were students who were 10 times sharper than me. I almost doubted my abilities after comparing myself to them, but **I made the decision to invest in myself.** Rather than hate or envy fellow students who I perceived to be "better" than me, I decided to pursue opportunities that would enhance my skills to BE a better me. I decided to put my time in! I took control of who I desired to BE. I used search engines and I met with professors and staff in our Career Development and Service Learning Office to seek internship opportunities. I was always amongst the first to submit applications or to indicate an interest in attending professional development opportunities. There were times when I paid for my own professional development. I secured a paid internship every summer and attended every conference I could. **Don't hate, elevate!**

Being open-minded opened new doors for me. A life-changing moment occurred during my internship experience at NASA Space Center-Langley in Hampton, Virginia during the summer of 2005. This was a Science, Technology, Engineering, and Mathematics (STEM) program geared towards cultivating future teachers into STEM education. To be honest, I had no intentions of pursuing STEM education as a career. However, I felt that I could benefit from the exposure and content embedded in the experience the internship offered. I was correct! I thought I was advanced and prepared to conquer anything. I was—from my perspective, until I was tasked with building lesson plans and completing projects on a Mac computer. I had never operated a Mac. I was a Windows guru. Guess what? I learned it.

I googled and watched a plethora of YouTube videos to learn how to navigate my MacBook. My classmate at the time, Breslin Stevenson owned a MacBook. He mentored me and showed me the ropes. Since then, I have only owned Mac computers. I BEcame a better person as a result of **my decision** to invest in myself. I developed new skills, friendships, connections, and knowledge because I was willing to BE open-minded. My only regret is that I wish I'd known then that I was cultivated on the grounds where the "hidden figures," Katherine Johnson, Mary Jackson, and Dorothy Vaughan blazed a trail of excellence. This is why I advocate for culturally relevant teaching. Their stories should have been an integral part of the curriculum during that internship and in every classroom. However, when I did learn about the hidden figures, it reified my why and my who! It reminded me that Black excellence is in my DNA, in spite of the stories, truths, and figures "hidden" from mainstream knowledge.

To BE better, you have to make up in your mind that you are worth better and you deserve better. I made the decision to BE better.

Better won't come unless you're grateful for what you have.
Better won't come unless you make the jump to get it!

Better is within you! You have to see the jump that you make as an investment towards BEing a better you. Go get your blessing!

Think as a Winner

Your mindset drives your responses to challenges. People often say think like a winner. You are already a winner, so think as one! You can overcome the **doubts** of everything that could go wrong by demolishing negative thoughts with the possibilities of everything that could go right! Sometimes you have to teach yourself who you can become! Society has played so many tricks on our minds that sometimes we have to teach our minds by manifesting things we never imagine ourselves doing. Watch me work! Look in the mirror and tell yourself, "It's time to eat!" **It's time to feed your hunger for growth, but you need to stop feeding yourself the same things expecting a different outcome. That's insanity.** There is so much the world has to offer, but our closed-minds are limiting us from experiencing the greatness that life has to offer. Try new things even when you have **doubts** that you may not like it. Overcome your doubts by ignoring those voices in your head. Just do it.

Just JUMP! Forget what others think.
Forget what could go wrong.
Speak back to those voices in your head and just jump!
Jump into new territories! Jump into greatness!
Jump over doubt and into new possibilities!

BE Optimistic

Being open-minded inspires us to BE optimistic. What do you have to lose by BEing optimistic? I mean, what do you have to lose if you thought positively? Because of the power invested in you, you have the ability to verbalize your destiny. You have the ability to speak and manifest visions because of the God in you. If you believe that you will BE unsuccessful, your actions and decisions will align with that belief.

The game, Uno presents many teachable moments. I have almost lost friends and family over some of the decisions I've made during the game. If you have never played Uno, please research it and try it out. Those who have played Uno can attest to the level of betrayal they felt when their friend or family member dropped a "draw four" on the table and they had to draw four cards, which prolonged their duration in the game. With Uno, the object of the game is to get down to one card, call "Uno" and call "out" to BE out of the game, if your card aligns with the criteria of the card that is placed on the table.

Things get worse because as you play with different people, they have different rules for the game. For instance, in my crew, we play "stacks" and "triples." When stacking, I can drop a stack of 4 draw 4's on the table and the person next to me would have to draw 16 cards! When I'm in that position, I always get slightly upset, especially if I was down to two cards. However, I have seen players who collected a whole hand of cards with a smile. I witnessed one player who we intentionally kept stacking "draw 4's" on say, "That's fine. I'ma show y'all something." He had a positive mindset. He was strategic in how he played his cards. He used his circumstance as a "teachable moment." By the end of the game, he was "out" and we were still in the game. We played him, but he ended up playing us. Remember, life isn't about the cards you've been dealt, but how and when you play your cards. BE optimistic!

What I learned from this experience was:

- **Don't take it personally:** It's a game. Remember you must learn to have fun in life. Everything isn't serious. Don't take everything to heart.

- **Don't panic:** Keep calm. Don't doubt your ability to overcome the situation. Remain calm and declare that you will rebound. You have to BE optimistic.

- **Work with what you have:** Look at what you have and strategize to work it to your advantage. You must also organize to see what you are working with. It is easier to make decisions when you are organized.

- **Pay attention to others:** If you pay attention to the cards others are putting down, you will know how to play your cards. Sometimes, minding someone else's business will work in your favor. You have to BE attentive to predict how other players will move. The moral of the story is, watch people!

- **There is power in the WAIT:** Don't drop all of your cards at once! You have to BE strategic. Play your cards at the right time. Don't ever let your right hand know what your left hand is doing.

- **Understand why it worked:** You won because you had a winning mindset. You responded well to a minor setback and you strategized. Had you allowed **doubt** to win, there's no doubt you would've lost the game.

Optimism beats pessimism any day. The pessimist is typically stuck on everything that's going wrong. Their focus and energy is channeled towards the negatives, which may limit them from moving forward. When all we see is negativity, it can BE hard to move forward. For instance, the pessimist will encounter a challenge and begin to focus on what they can't do as a result of the challenge. Like the Uno scenario, there is much we can learn about how people respond to situations.

BEing Optimistic For Your Team

A team of ants are marching to snack on a nearby doughnut. However, there is a puddle of water that separates the ants from the doughnut. The pessimistic ant says that there's no point in trying to get the doughnut because they'd drown trying to get to it. However, the optimistic ant searches for opportunities. The ant finds a nearby leaf and decides to use the leaf as a boat to get to the doughnut. It worked! Don't focus on your problems. Focus on solutions.

Challenging times aren't the moments when you should strike out, you should strike in and strategize!

Outweigh all of your options. Most times you won't have all the answers, so you should connect with optimistic people! They will support you in engaging in optimism. They will remind you when doubt creeps in to not BE sidetracked by minor or major setbacks or delays.

A Delay is a Temporary Denial

People often proclaim that "a delay is not a denial." That's not always true. Realistically speaking, **a delay is a denial—a temporary one.** The reality is we will BE denied from things and people that do not align with our purpose. Similarly, we will BE denied things and opportunities that do not *yet* align with our purpose. If you have not done so already, supplement the power of your vocabulary by injecting the word 'yet' in any statement that capitalizes on negativity. You have to begin countering negativity with positivity, which begins with what you say, how you say it, and what you allow to BE proclaimed to you!

You can't swim....

I can't swim **yet.**

You don't have a car.

I don't have a car **yet.**

You haven't completed your master's degree.

I have not completed my master's degree **yet.**

You're not on the Dean's list.

I am not on the Dean's list **yet.**

When you focus on problems, you will have more problems. When you focus on possibilities, you will have more opportunities. Focus on the possibilities as much as you focus on your problems! Apply that same energy towards your possibilities.

You'll find a purpose connected to every problem. Your purpose is to BE the answer to a problem here on this Earth. Find out what the problem is and have the optimism to know that you are not the problem, you are the answer. You may have problems, but you are not what you experience. Don't allow anyone to tell you are a problem. Remember who you are. BE optimistic in knowing that whatever you desire, you will acquire! You may not see it yet, but it's coming in due time. **"BE not weary in well doing for in due season you shall reap if you faint not" (Galatians 6:9).**

Check Your Feelings

When I hear people say, "I feel like a failure," I remind them that our feelings do not depict our identities. Our feelings indicate our current emotional state. For instance, people often say, "I'm tired." You may FEEL tired, but you are not tired. That is not who you are, but rather your current emotional state. Remember, when you say I AM, you are exerting the God power within you. You become what you think, believe, and speak. Some people also say, "I'm lonely." You may FEEL alone, but loneliness isn't your identity; it is only your current emotional state. What you feel is legitimate. The reality is that sometimes we give too much power into what we feel without regard to our possible blind spots. You may FEEL lonely, but did you think of how many calls you rejected today and how many text messages you didn't respond to? Sometimes we have to reframe our thoughts and BE cautious not to BE too caught up into our emotions. Your feelings are caused by your thoughts, which is your perception of your reality. This is why you have to BE optimistic and remember that your feelings don't define you!

Optimism releases endorphins, which are the feel-good hormones in your body. If you want to experience success and happiness, anticipate the various trials and tribulations that will precede the triumph, and *know* without a **doubt that you will BE victorious.**

Do things that release endorphins, by any means necessary.

CHAPTER 3

BE ACCOUNTABLE

BE ACCOUNTABLE

"You cannot control or change all circumstances and situations; but you must BE accountable for the things your calling has to account for"

– Anthony Broughton

You must take personal responsibility. You cannot change the circumstances, the seasons, or the wind, but you can change yourself. That is something you have charge of.

– Jim Rohn

If you hang out with chickens, you're going to cluck and if you hang out with eagle, you're going to fly.

– Steve Maraboli

Affirmation: I will overcome doubting my ability to answer my calling.

When you elevate you will have elevated responsibility.

The higher you fly the more turbulence you'll experience.

Your elevation comes with a cost!

You will have to make numerous, ongoing sacrifices to maintain your accountability. You will have to choose commitment over comfort. There will be many long hours, sacrifices, blood, sweat, and tears in your new position. In fact, you can expect to BE called upon at the most inconvenient times. You will have to respond to problems as they arise at any given time. Why are you complaining? Didn't you pray or ask for this? Didn't you want to be a supervisor? **BE careful what you pray for!** You will learn more about the burden of elevation in Chapter 5 on page 88.

You may not BE qualified according to human-constructed criteria to perform the job at hand, but God qualifies the called. No, you may not feel like you currently possess the prerequisite skills to perform the job, but if you dared to step out on faith, dare to walk into your calling. You must take responsibility for the people who now depend on your "leadership." The **"teachable moment"** is, don't step forward if you are not *willing* to BE accountable. Come correct or have a seat! In the words of my grandmother, "Don't ask for food if you're not going to eat it." If you're not going to BE accountable, don't **account** for more than you're **able** to yet handle with care.

Your decisions are not solely about you. There are lives at stake. Every decision you make will impact the world on a larger scale. You may not see it yet, but your impact is more comprehensive than you'll ever know. There are no assessments that can measure the true magnitude of your impact. The truth is, only God sees and knows your **true** impact. Even then, the world can't compensate you for your impact, because your worth and your work are priceless if you're doing God's work.

RESPECT THE PROCESS

You will hear it time after time throughout this book to **respect the process.** If you submit to the process, your current position should build and cultivate you for the next level. You are not in your position to simply **exist** (noun); you must also **BE** (verb). Yes, you may BE in an entry-level position; yes, you may BE 'just' an assistant; yes, you may BE 'just' a custodian, but "do not despise these small beginnings" (Zechariah 4:10). BE great in your 'little' position, so you can thrive in your 'big' position. Do not underestimate the teachable moments you will learn through this process. It may seem like a "small" beginning, but small things can make a big impact. If you take your experience seriously and operate passionately during your "small beginnings," you will develop the experiential knowledge that will benefit you in your next chapter. For instance, my experiences as a student, certified teacher, and center administrator all inform my work as a professor. I know what it's like to be in the trenches, so I can make informed decisions and equip my students with the skills and knowledge they need to BE successful. Too often, our society has allowed people to occupy seats of power and to make uninformed decisions with no experience in the field they're leading. How can you make decisions for an entire education system and you've never taught? How can you tell teachers what and how to teach and you've never taught a classroom of students? How can you tell surgeons how they should BE performing surgeries if you have never worked in an operating room?

BE faithful over a few things, so you can BE ruler over many things! (Matthew 25:23). Master your current work. Work on BEing the best at what you do, right now! As long as you have breath in your body and blood running warm in your veins, you should strive to do your best and BE the best in whatever you do. In the words of Reverend Dr. Martin Luther King, Jr during his speech on October 26, 1967 to a group of students at Barratt Junior High School in Philadelphia,

"If it falls your lot to BE a street sweeper, sweep streets like Michelangelo painted pictures, sweep streets like Beethoven composed music, sweep streets like Leontyne Price sings before the Metropolitan Opera. Sweep streets like Shakespeare wrote poetry. Sweep streets so well that all the hosts of heaven and earth will have to pause and say: Here lived a great street sweeper who swept his job well. If you can't BE a pine at the top of the hill, BE a shrub in the valley. BE the best little shrub on the side of the hill. BE a bush if you can't BE a tree. If you can't BE a highway, just BE a trail. If you can't BE a sun, BE a star. For it isn't by size that you win or fail. BE the best of whatever you are."

Regardless of whether or not you chose to BE, you are **accountable** for BEing a better you. You are accountable for your actions, your impact on others, the advancement of the company, and for answering the call of the responsibilities (not just the "job") **you** prayed and signed up for.

So, where do you go from here? You may feel lost or unsure of where you went wrong or where to begin in the process of BEing better. I've learned that influences impact your journey to BEing a better you. In the word influence, I hear the word **flew**. Sometimes during our flight of life, we have to take an **in**ventory of who **flew** with us to get to where we are and examine who is currently in our flock. Someone in your flock should BE able to support you in growth. Is your flock holding you accountable for BEing a better you? Is your flock seeking to fly higher?

Do Birds of a Feather Truly Flock Together?

The higher you elevate, the more you have to eliminate. They say that birds of a feather flock together. If I could select a bird that best represents me, I'd select an eagle. I've admired eagles for their size, beauty, and abilities since I was a child, watching an episode about eagles on the Discovery Channel. After reflecting, although I valued having a diverse flock theoretically, the altitude that birds are able to fly changed my perspective. For instance, eagles exert little effort to fly at approximately 10,000 feet while most birds fly relatively low around 500 feet, unless they are in migration. Like birds, we flock or hang with like-minded people as we flock through life. Unfortunately, if you are an eagle, you will eventually find yourself alone or with other eagles the higher you begin to fly. Other birds seek shelter to avoid the rain, while eagles fly above the clouds instead. I am not inferring that eagles are "better" than other birds, but other birds do not possess the capacity to face the store and elevate as eagles do.

Like the eagle, I found myself alone as I elevated to higher altitudes. It's hard to admit, but this is my reality. I lost several "friends" along my journey. As a result, I do not call just anyone my friend, bro, or sis. I call such people acquaintances. No, I'm perfect. I make mistakes and I have done things I regretted, but I've come to realize that only people—or birds of my feather are still flocking with me today. My friends checked me when I was wrong and fought to reconcile our issues, rather than flocking away! However, if many of us look back over our lives, we may notice that several people who originally flocked with us are no longer apart of the flock. They left us as we soared to new altitudes of our lives, or we left them to "fly high when they go low," in the words of our former first Lady Michelle Obama.

The point is, everyone does not possess the capacity to soar with you; and everyone does not deserve the privilege to join you at your next level. While we may think this lack of capacity to soar with you is solely because of their personality, I've learned that the values, perspectives, and mindsets of people who no longer soar with me are no longer aligned to mine. At one point in my life, I thought our values, perspectives, mindsets, and purposes were aligned. At one point, I could flock to the club and have a good time without worrying about someone going live and recording me with "my drank and my two step." At one point, I thought I could post whatever content I desired because it was "my" social media. At one point, I could afford to go out and party all night and splurge during out-of-town weekend trips, but then things changed.

YOUR CALLING IS CALLING YOU

Things changed drastically the moment I chose to finally **BE accountable** for answering my calling. I learned that your calling will keep calling you until you answer. I flocked away from my calling, passion, and my ability to operate at my fullest capacity because of distractions and **doubt**. Unfortunately, my acquaintances were not supportive when I answered my call. They thought me pursuing my doctorate was "too soon." Before we'd go out or even times when we were commuting to the club or to an event, they'd make little slick comments while I was trying to get my paper in by the 11:59 deadline. Had I listened to them, I would not have earned my doctorate by the age of 30. I sacrificed then for what I have now. All I have to say is don't knock someone who's trying to do their thing. Support them. Everyone will choose their own pathway. Let them BE great in whatever pathway they choose. A doctorate isn't for everyone, but don't stop me because you don't see the vision!

I became a "new" person when I began to take accountability for answering my calling. I no longer felt comfortable posting just any picture on social media, because I began to see myself as a "brand." My new perspective and newly aligning behavior as a result of answering my calling made my acquaintances upset. They felt like I "changed." Yes, I did. How can you expect me to grow and not change? Growth in general requires physical and intellectual **changes**. You cannot fly at higher altitudes without developing the strength and skills required. I had to develop bigger muscles to move mountains. I knew I could move mountains because I was inspired by people who were bigger and better.

I learned from eagles who were veteran flyers. My mentors would swoop down and tell me, "come with us now!" My mentors and elders held me to a higher standard. I saw what they consumed and realized that I needed to try their regimen. If you want to BE better you have to watch what "BETTER" people do. Metaphorically, my mentors ate bigger things than I was accustomed to. While I was eating mealworms and seeds, they were eating squirrels, prairies dogs, raccoons, rabbits, and other birds. I could not grow to my fullest capacity because I was not consuming the things that could elevate me.

I was not consuming literature or engaging in professional or personal development that challenged me. I was not interfacing with a variety of people with varied levels of experiences, knowledge, and perspectives that could edify me. I was not in spaces that aligned with my calling. I stepped into rooms where I **doubted** my abilities to articulate my ideas and demonstrate my skills. I slept on my gift. I kept it to myself. I played around with my calling, keeping it on "do not disturb." I attempted to avoid **BE**ing **accountable** for answering who God called me to BE. However, my mentors helped me to recognize the commitments I needed to make to BEcome the greatest version of myself!

I had to make a choice. If those who flock with me aren't willing to grow, I'll naturally outgrow them if I allow God to order my steps. I would no longer 'fit' in, and that's ok. I would no longer BE fit for a chicken coop. I had to spread my wings and mount up like an eagle. I thought I was waiting on the Lord, but the Lord was waiting on me! I had to trust the process of BEcoming accountable for my future. I had to manifest the vision God gave me, regardless of what others thought and how they felt. If God called me to BE an eagle, I'm no longer clipping my wings to make others feel comfortable. I will not take my gift to the grave.

So many people leave this world without fulfilling the highest expression of themselves. No matter what you do, people will make their own choices. I've learned that when they see you soaring high, although they chose to go low, they may perceive it as **shade.** They are correct. It is shade, which is provided by the shadow of your large wings soaring high in the light. It will remain shade until they chose to soar with you, not beneath you. That's their choice, not yours. You are not responsible for the choices they make, but you have to **BE accountable** for yours. Likewise, you are not accountable for the shade they choose to soar under. That's their choice. **Your greatest test will BE how you handle people who mishandle you. Don't swoop to their level. Swoop above and teach them!**

Give Back: BE an Educating Mentor

Dr. Maya Angelou said, "When you learn, teach. When you get, give." We must BE accountable for our duty to give back. As an educator my role as a mentor became quite natural. In fact, the "highly acclaimed" Call Me M.I.S.T.E.R. program inspired me to BE a mentor. The acronym M.I.S.T.E.R. represents Mentors Inspiring Students Towards Effective Role models. I've learned that there are positive and negative mentors in our lives. The mentors who have been most effective in my life are those who operated in an educator capacity. My role as a mentor is to scaffold or to support my mentee in BEing their best selves. As a result I work to hold them accountable to BE who they are called to be. Mentors are not perfect. However, we must BE accountable for using the "teachable moments" of our lives, their lives, and the lives of others to educate our mentees and ourselves in the process. Thus, whatever I learn, I teach. Whatever I get, I give. It's up to our mentees to do what they want with it. You can lead a horse to the water, but you can't make him drink. The hard reality is, you can't save everyone. It is not your job to do so. In the words of my grandmother, "Do what you can do."

Some of my most impactful mentoring has occurred as a result of my mentees doing what they want, and learning from their own experiences. Some people must touch the stove to know it's hot. Our roles as educating mentors is to ensure our mentees don't miss the "teachable moment" embedded in their experiences. We must support them in identifying tools and approaches to use for future experiences. Otherwise, the school of life will make them repeat the course. Mentees will not always follow your recommendations. I've learned that we cannot BE selfish as mentors. We cannot infringe our beliefs and approaches on our mentees. It is still their life to live – not ours. We've had our times! They will need to have theirs. No, you don't want them to repeat some of your decisions in life, but perhaps they need to. Maybe they need to learn for themselves? Then they can appreciate your role as a trusted guide or in their life. Then they can honor your feedback, because they now know (based on their experience) that you know what you are talking about. Mentors must also realize that their mentees can also mentor them. Let that sink in.

"IF YOU FAIL TO ADEQUATELY PREPARE,
YOU ARE PREPARING TO FAIL OR BE FAILED."

Put Your Time In

In the words of the old folk, "You have to put your time in." BEing prepared is one of the easiest lessons I learned, because lack of preparation taught me! There were times when I felt embarrassed, because I wasn't prepared. I recall teachers and professors putting me on the spot to answer questions and I wasn't prepared to respond. I would get upset and defensive, wondering why would they embarrass me like that? Then, I checked myself and challenged myself to **BE**come **accountable** for my actions by asking myself, why was I not prepared? Experiencing embarrassment inspired me to invest in adequate preparation. Abraham Lincoln once stated, "Give me six hours to chop down a tree and I will spend the first four sharpening the axe." We have to trust the process and BE strategic in how we spend our time. BEing prepared is not convenient, but it is essential. We can't blame others because we failed to prepare. In fact, we put more stress on ourselves if we do not take the time to prepare for the things we can prepare for. **If you stay ready you won't have to get ready.** The following strategies has helped me BE prepared:

- **BE petty.** *Don't come for me unless I send for you.* #screenshot.

Yes, keep your receipts. Keep your documentation at all times. You have to BE prepared to defend yourself if necessary, because #whatyounotgone'dois come for me.

- **Do your homework!** That's self-explanatory. Always do your research. Take the time to read.

- **Seek help.** *Tap into the power of experiential knowledge.* Efficient planning requires that you have the knowledge to think the "right" thoughts and ask the "right" questions. The "right" thoughts and questions depends upon the content and context of what you are planning. You can plan to feed 50 people at the banquet. You "know" that everyone will want either chicken or beef with mashed potatoes and asparagus. You have a guest that shows up and states the menu options did not include a vegan option. There are also people who complained that they do not eat asparagus. There was not an option for people to indicate their food restrictions on the invitation. If you consulted with an event planner who had the knowledge, you would have learned the "right" questions to ask. Sometimes you are not the best person to plan certain things. Solicit help when planning so you are not wasting time. Save yourself the embarrassment.

- **Have back up plans.** Always have a plan B, C, and D.

When deepening your knowledge consider the various variables. Don't expect the "worst," but do not expect things to go 100% as planned. What if things go wrong? What are the risks? What are the liabilities? What are the threats? How can you prepare for them? This is why the education process is essential. You have to do your homework, but you should have your homework checked by a mentor. You do not have all power in your hands. You do not get to control the game. However, you can control your moves on the board, while influencing the moves of others.

- **Engage in efficient exercises**

Practice doesn't make perfect. Perfection is fictitious. Efficient practice produces proficiency. If you exercise with a coach, you may learn that you're practicing or performing an exercise ineffectively. **Sometimes we can do the right exercise with the wrong form**! Be efficient in what you do.

- **BE consistent** in your preparation. (See Chapter 6)

- **Execute with precision**. Don't let your preparation BE in vain. Strike while the iron is hot. You must BE ready to apply your knowledge and skills when necessary. If you are not prepared to strike while the iron is hot you may miss the opportunity of a lifetime.

- **BE organized.** Sometimes we don't know what we have.

I have bought two of the same shirts because I was not organized. Having physical order will help you have mental order. When it's time to fight you don't have time to go searching for your weapon. You need to know where it is, so you can strike!

Your enemies are prepared

There's a song in the Disney movie, *Lion King* called "BE prepared." This song is sung by Scar, the villain who plotted to kill King Mufasa.In the song he says, "So prepare for the coup of the century. BE prepared for the murkiest scam. Meticulous planning." This is an example of how there are people meticulously planning to work against you. In fact, there are people who are plotting and planning to destroy you! They are passionately preparing for your defeat with every fiber of their BEing. Let them dig their own grave.

If you fail to prepare your enemies will prepare to celebrate your failure. Each second you put it off is a second that someone else will put on. If you don't have to manifest that idea or dream you've been sitting on, someone else will. More importantly, if you don't stop telling your frienemies your business, when you look up again, they'll be profiting off the same idea they told you was a "bad idea." Fortunately, no one can duplicate and execute the vision that God gave you!

BE ACCOUNTABLE For Your Actions

Let's face it, owning up to some of the decisions we've made can BE a tough pill to swallow. We must muster up the courage to admit when we're wrong. In a nutshell, we have to BE accountable for our actions. We can't expect to simply get away with how we treat people. There's a price to pay whether or not you chose to BE accountable for your actions. Karma does exist. If you mistreat people, it will come back to you. What you put out into the universe will return to you. BE careful how you treat people. Typically, you do not want to burn bridges. You never know where life will lead you. You may end up needing that person again. However, there are bridges that you do need to burn, but BE careful how you burn them and why you burn them. As you will learn later on in this book, sometimes there is a good in good bye. Own your stuff! Own your truth! Own your mistakes! Own your choices! Own your stuff! People will throw your stuff in your face, but acknowledge it! People will magnify your mistakes and put it on auto play. However, when you own your stuff or when you are accountable for your stuff, there is nothing else others can do about it. Once you acknowledge your likelihood to make "mistakes," you shatter your own glass ceiling of perfection. No one is perfect. We all make decisions we regret for various reasons. However, if you do not learn from your experiences, you are bound to impede your process of BEing a better you. You can't BE who you are without owning the stuff that makes you who you are. If people don't like it, that's their business. They should be worried about their own "stuff". Sometimes people are struggling with the same thing they keep throwing in your face.

Accountability is a bold choice. It's easy to neglect obligations. It's easy to just walk away. Demolish doubt! Face your fears! Look your troubles and worries in the face and say, "I've got this!" #BEempowered

-Anthony Broughton

CHAPTER 4

BE STUDIOUS

CHAPTER 4
BE STUDIOUS

*"Education is not the filling of the pail,
but the lighting of a fire."*

-William Butler Yeats

Affirmation: I will overcome doubting my potential as the key player in my educational journey.

Redefine and revolutionize "education"

" Until the story of the hunt is told by the lion, the tale of the hunt will always glorify the hunter, "is an African proverb that reminds me there is much power in not only who is telling a story, but also from what perspective they are telling it. This quote parallels with what Chimamanda Nozi Adichei (2009, July) cautioned as "the danger of a single story." So, I'm going to tell my story, because my story is an essential part of BEING a BETTER me. I encourage you to tell yours as well. Always remember there is power in owning and telling your story! My process of redefining education began with taking accountability for my learning. I began by seeking to reclaim access to knowledge that was stolen, destroyed, and manipulated by colonizers. African diasporic literacy is not mainstream information. Read the book, *African Diasporic Literacy: The Heart of Transformation in K-12 Schools and Teacher Education* by Gloria Boutte, Lamar Johnson, Gwenda Greene and Dywanna Smith for more information. I tell my story because you never know who will BE inspired to BE better as a result of your vulnerability to share your story. Let me forewarn you, I'm about to be transparent. Education is near and dear to my heart, but there is a dark side that I must share. You may not agree with what I'm about to say and how I say it. Some things may offend you, but I want to remind you to remember to **BE open-minded** as examined in Chapter 2. However, speaking this truth is the most essential aspect of me BEing a DOUBT DEMOLISHER.

Education as Defined and Enforced by Whom?

While we think we are learning the truth, we may be learning someone else's truth. For every story there is a counter story. For instance, I learned the Christopher Columbus discovered America. That's a single story, but what would we learn from the Native American perspective, which was not accurately portrayed in school curricula? What would we learn from the African perspective? You can't discover something that was already occupied. However, this single story was taught and we learned it. We have to BE careful not to buy into single stories. The traditional process of schooling and mass media has taught me one perspective in most cases—the White, middle class perspective. This is why I draw from counter-stories of Black excellence. Hearing the great contributions of my ancestors played and still plays an integral role in BEing a better me. This is why I've chosen to BE a counter story, because I want to inspire others for generations to come, as someone's future ancestor. That's one reason I decided to BE an educator! I've learned to question what I read and hear. It seems like a simple concept, but if that were the case school curricula would help develop our critical consciousness to become critical scholars, but most do not. So, when reading textbooks or any form of scholarship, I always do my own research and check other sources. If you fail to BE studious you'll easily compromise your organic greatness and lose yourself in the schooling process.

Grades and Degrees Don't Define You.

You can have ten thousand degrees, but lack common sense. You can be valedictorian, but if you need honors and awards to validate you, you've successfully mastered the art of assimilating to the norms, customs, and values of "The American Education System." You have demonstrated intelligence as narrowly defined by many as "academic achievement." Life has to mean more than simply achieving "degrees" while acquiring "knowledge" from others. What good is being "intelligent" if you do not possess the consciousness to empower yourself in the process. What good is having a degree if you dysconsciously or consciously perpetuate systemic racism by miseducating others with the miseducation you've been fed? This is why we have to BE better by raising our consciousness to re-define education. **If you don't know, now you know.** You will loose yourself embracing someone else's "education." You have the power to define education for yourself!

Re-defining Education

> "Consciousness (literally translated to mean with knowledge or knowing others) is the internal manifestation of knowledge. Awareness is the distinguishing quality that differentiates between human life that is functional and life that is dysfunctional. As people's shared knowledge is the criteria for assessing their level of civilization, personal awareness the way by which we determine individual function. There is no wonder that the Ancient African people taught the world (and later transmitted by the Greek and Roman students of Africa) that the ultimate instruction for human growth and transformation was: "Man know they self" To BE conscious was to BE alive and BE human. (p.vi, Na'im Akbar, 1998 in the book entitled, *Know Thyself*)

We must re-define education for ourselves. A ***real education*** is edifying, liberating, humanizing, empowering, transformational, and rewarding. If it is not, it is what Dr. Carter G. Woodson described back in 1935 as mis-education. Education should cultivate the process of drawing out your potential. It should give you life, not death. It should give you joy, not sorrow. Education should light your fire, not shun you into a murky cold pit of self-**doubt.** Education should help you discover who you are, not solely what you desire to BE. Education should show you who can BE, not who can't BE. It should capitalize on your strengths, and inspire you to cultivate your areas for growth. To access this type of education, we must **BE Studious**.

Webster's dictionary defined studious as "assiduous in the pursuit of learning." Admittedly, every time I hear the word study, I think of school. In my mind, I envision paper, a pencil, highlighters, notebooks, and now my laptop. When I was younger, encyclopedias would BE included on that list. Originally education for me was something I went to school to obtain. Most teachers and professors made it clear that they were equipped with *the* knowledge that I needed to obtain, study, and regurgitate. Many teachers, who I perceived as "bearers of knowledge" would often say, "I have mine. You need to get yours." In my mind I would think to myself, "You have your what?" Years later, I now know what that 'what' is. They obtained *their* educational credentials and I needed to work hard to earn mine. So, now that I have my little degree and think I know so much (lol), as the people would say, I'd like to take this point of privilege to say, "Yes, I do know so much with my *little* degree". Although, I don't know it all, I do know now that "getting an education" without developing critical conscious was a waste of my time. There, I said it. (Drops mic and exits stage left.)

Let's face it, America's educational system was never designed for Black and Brown people. Do your research. You don't have to take my word for it. The proof is in the pudding. Eugenics and its role in education with regard to standardized testing (which we still use today, by the way) was designed to "prove" Black inferiority with culturally biased tests. The process of schooling has historically and traditionally shoved an Eurocentric curriculum down our throats, while in the same breath saying "Education for all." If you are reading this and you disagree or this doesn't speak to your reality, this is an opportunity to BE open-minded. Again, there will be moments when you feel uncomfortable grappling with other people's truths; however, these moments are essential to BEing better in our pursuit of BEcoming better.

THE "DISENGAGED"

I was in one of the most unenthusiastic teacher's class when I asked, "When am I going to use these formulas in real life?" She responded, "Don't ask questions. Just do it." That's when I learned that school could BE a form of slavery. I spent the day picking content from textbooks and placing it in my learning bag to please the master, so I can become free when I get my degree. While that may sound harsh, it was how I internalized it; and my story matters. For many students, schooling can BE dehumanizing and deadly. No wonder why it is so easy for people to drop out, disconnect, and disengage from the process of schooling. Many teachers, administrators, policy-makers, and community members victimize students for displaying symptoms of an oppressive system. However, we need to look in the mirror.

The curriculum, as presented in most cases, will have you feeling like you are incapable, dumb, and "behind." **Some teachers will say that students are "disengaged," but perhaps their teaching is disengaging. We can't expect students to BE responsive to our curriculum, if the curriculum isn't responsive to our students.** People discuss and capitalize off the concept of an "educational achievement gap," but they won't discuss the educational debt (Gloria Ladson-Billings), the opportunity gap (Dr. Linda Darling-Hamond), and the attitude gap (Baruti Kafele). Again, a *real* education doesn't produce or normalize educational achievement gaps. This is why I'm grateful for real educators who helped me redefine education. They helped me realize that being street smart (possessing the ability to apply content to real-life situations), was just as important as being book smart. What good is an education if it's not going to benefit you in the "real world?"

Real Educators

In spite of me feeling like "getting an education" was a waste of time, there were educators who cultivated my interests, gifts, and talents in ways that helped me to manifest what I now define as a *real education*. These educators spoke life into my **BE**ing and helped me to see the value of a *real education*. Their words of power and inspiration supported me in **demolishing all doubts** during my educational journey. Their innovative, culturally relevant approaches connected with my realities. They helped me apply content to my personal life, which generated within me an appreciation for *real education*. Real educators helped me to discover that a real education should BE a process of self-discovery and collective evolution, not simply information to BE memorized. They loved and cared for me in the classroom as if I were their own. They ensured that I was challenged through a curriculum that reflected the contributions of Black and Brown people. They made it clear through the curriculum that I embodied and will continue to embody Black excellence. I saw myself in books, posters, materials, history, and assignments beyond Black History Month.

My real educators who were both Black and White, possessed what I longed for in an educational setting! In their classrooms, it didn't feel like slavery because I wasn't doing work for them, I was doing work for myself. I learned life skills in those classrooms, and that's when I realized the transformative power of a *real education*. William Arthur Ward was spot on when he said, "The mediocre teacher tells. The good teacher explains. The superior teacher demonstrates. The great teacher inspires." Learn from those who inspire you as well as though who aspire to see you fail. We can even learn from the mediocre teachers why we shouldn't BE mediocre. There is a teacher and a lesson in every situation, if we are **studious.**

Education is not the filling of the pail,
but the lighting of a fire.
-William Butler Yeats

Life has taught me that there is a distinction between what we have traditionally referred to as "teachers" and "educators." Although used interchangeably, I have learned that these two titles and roles are not synonymous. A teacher imparts knowledge to students. However, an educator possesses the gift and ability to foster meaningful relationships in ways that draw out students' potential. *Educares,* which is the Latin word for education means to draw out. Educators don't seek to "fill" your pail. Educators light your fire and inspires you to BE better in the process.

Educational data demonstrates that although *teachers* pass teacher examinations, many of them are unable to foster learning in ways that produce favorable outcomes for *all* students. *Educators* are student-centered and operate out of their motherly or fatherly love for their students. Although most *educators* hold teaching licenses, some do not because of institutionalized racism (i.e., culturally biased tests, Eugenics), and others don't need it because they were called to educate beyond the realms of traditional classroom spaces. What life has taught me is that everyone and everything can BE a teacher. The world is our classroom and life itself is full of teachers who engage in God's work by facilitating "teachable moments" through life's curriculum. To date, my grandmother, who did not possess a "teaching license" as defined by societal norms was one of the best educators that I've encountered.

BEing Accountable

I know many people who simply want a doctorate so that people can call them "Dr." I'm here to tell you that with the title comes great **accountability**. You will be held accountable for what you do with your knowledge. In the words of my academic mother, Dr. Gloria Boutte, "COME CORRECT!" If you want to BE called "Dr," BE prepared to respond to the expectations that are attached to the title. People will come for you! People will come for your credentials! "Oh, did you see he misspelled that word in his post? Doesn't he have a doctorate?" "Didn't he get his degree from that online school?" "Is that school even credible?" "So, tell me about...?" Yes, people will interrogate you and thereafter form negative perceptions about your skills and the quality of the institution you attended if you cannot show what you know.

However, I've learned that no matter where you earn your degree, you must maximize the moment. **Being studious helps** to deepen your knowledge and enhance your skills. **People should feel the degree of your degree. They should feel the passion burning**

within you by being in your presence. Your presence then has the capacity to inspire others to BE better. Yes, people should put some respect on your name by addressing you by your title, when appropriate, but you should put some respect on your own name first. Ensure that you have the academic integrity, the self-knowledge, the character, and the capacity to **BE accountable for your title**. People can respect your title if you **serve** with it. Some people see my doctorate and perceive it as success. For me, the "success" was the person I BEcame through the process. I want to underscore that no matter where you are in your educational journey, make every moment matter! Take advantage of every opportunity to learn and grow. Degrees are measured by course completion and credit hours. Each chapter of our lives provides us opportunities to be awarded credit hours for the knowledge we've gained during our experiences. How many credit hours did you earn in the school of life this week? Did you maximize the moment?

Therefore, as you seek to advance yourself in the field of education, you must make a conscious effort to BE strategic and intentional about where, how, and why you advance your education. Don't pursue degrees or attend schools for titles. You should factor in how the degree and the institution will cultivate your journey to BE as you are becoming a better you.

You are accountable for what
you do with your education.

When I entered my doctoral program, I was introduced to scholarly literature by Dr. Gloria Boutte, my academic mother, and Dr. Susi Long. The works of culturally relevant pedagogy, critical race theory, and African Diasporic literacy, exposed me to transform my thinking. This process shifted my thinking and how I viewed education. I became a member of the University of South Carolina Center for the Excellence and Equity of African American Students, where I was able to grow amongst like-minded scholars. **Once you know better, you should chose to do and BE better.** This work takes courage, passion, and a relentless commitment to the excellence and equity of Black children. **It requires you to unapologetically speak truth to power! Education should help you make a positive impact on the world.**

What good is it to have degrees, and you are one, two, or three degrees hotter, but no one feels your impact? You have to unlearn a lot of what you've been taught and replace it with new knowledge. I became **accountable** for **my *real* education.** I googled information I did not know. I sought various sources from various perspectives, rather than internalizing someone's knowledge as "the truth." I searched for YouTube videos that explained and demonstrated things I couldn't do. When I was in the presence of greatness or people in positions of power, I made an effort to learn from them. I asked questions to people who I thought would lead me to answers. Iron sharpens iron! I experienced and still experience "success," as a result of me taking full responsibility of **my learning.** It took a village to help me BEcome who I am today. You should take advantage of every opportunity that will cultivate your professional and personal development. Do not wait for someone to "give" you an education. You must define and co-create it with wise people. If you "take" education from others without analyzing it, it can dehumanize and control you. In the book, *The Miseducation of the Negro,* Dr. Carter G. Woodson said,

> "When you control a man's thinking you do not have to worry about his actions. You do not have to tell him not to stand here or go yonder. He will find his 'proper place' and will stay in it. You do not need to send him to the back door. He will go without being told. In fact, if there is no back door, he will cut one for his special benefit. His education makes it necessary."

Therefore, we must BE critical of what we internalize; because we BEcome what we believe.

Overcoming "Failure" in Education

Many students become stuck when they experience "failure." Where do you even begin when you're trying to "pick up" your grades? Midterms or progress reports can oftentimes jolt students into realizing they need to change and work harder to make improvements. However, it is difficult (not impossible) to rebound from an F to a B, or even an A overnight. Students in this boat should look at their temporary situation like a weight loss journey. Just because you've been working out intensely four days before the weigh in, doesn't mean you will see instant results. It takes time, consistency, perseverance, persistence, and a focused mind!

You can't expect to go hard after midterm and rebound with an A or B by the end of the semester. Yes, it is possible, but there are many variables at play. You may not BE able to see instant results with "academic achievement" as defined by society, but you can make the choice right now to change your attitude, which will change your character.

Your challenges don't just stem from your inability to earn the grades you desire. Your responses to your challenges are an invitation from life to change your character by shifting your thinking, which then shifts your actions. This is the process of a real education. A real education is when you are edified, inspired, fulfilled, and challenged to become better as a result of the content you consume. This is why we must BE careful and conscious about what content we consume and from whom. We must guard our heart and our ears from internalizing content from music, mass media, and others. We must BE critical of the sources of content knowledge. Otherwise, the "education" that we receive can mis-educate us in believing there's something wrong with us. We can be mis-educated to believe we are at-risk, deficit, or underachieving, when the reality may BE that we are resisting the norms of an educational system that has historically victimized, harmed, criminalize, and oppressed us. My argument is we must manifest education for ourselves. In spite of where you want to BE, you deserve to BE celebrated wherever you are in your process of BEing through transformational education. Where do you begin? How do you begin? I've learned that the best people to support you in this process are **real educators**, not teachers. Contact an educator who has positively impacted your life and thank them!

Again, this is my story. I survived, but I wish I was able to thrive during my schooling. What is your story? What does "education" mean to you? How can you advocate for equity in education? What's your role?

QUOTES

"The purpose of education is to educate each one of us to think critically and to think intensively. Intelligence plus character that is the goal of true education."   **-Dr. Martin Luther King, Jr.**

"Education is the movement from darkness to light."
– Allan Bloom

"Education is the most powerful weapon we can use to change the world." **– Nelson Mandella**

"Education is not preparation for life; education is life itself."
-John Dewey

"Education is a progressive discovery of our own ignorance."
- Will Durant

"Some people, unable to go to school, were more educated and more intelligent than college professors."
-Maya Angelou

"Let us think of education as the means of developing our greatest abilities, because in each of us there is a private hope and dream which, fulfilled, can BE translated into benefit for everyone and greater strength for our nation."
-John F. Kennedy

"Persistent questioning and healthy inquisitiveness are the first requisite for acquiring learning of any kind."
-Mahatma Gandhi

"By education, I mean an all-around drawing of the best in child and man in body, mind and spirit."
-Mahatma Gandhi

My Educational Plan

CHAPTER 5

BE SELF-CARING

CHAPTER 5
BE SELF-CARING

"Don't you ever for a second get to thinking you're irreplaceable."

-Beyoncé

"All of us are seeking the same thing. We share the desire to fulfill the highest, "Loving yourself has nothing to do with being selfish, self-centered or self-engrossed. It means that you accept yourself for what you are. Loving yourself means that you accept responsibility for your own development, growth and happiness."

-Iyanla Vanzant

Affirmation: I will overcome doubting my potential as the key player in my educational journey.

Many of us have heard flight attendants instruct us to put on our oxygen mask before helping others, in the event the cabin pressure changes. This is often used as a metaphor for self-care, which suggests that you should take care of yourself before worrying about others. This recommendation is based on an extreme emergency. We should not wait for extreme emergencies to BE self-caring. Self-caring must be a daily commitment. You will have to let some things and people go during this process! I don't know who needs to hear this but; cut it off! Let go of whatever you've been thinking about, worrying about, or struggling with. Don't second guess yourself. If your gut says cut it, CUT IT OFF! Our minds can BE like a closet full of clothes we haven't worn in years. We need to take an inventory and get rid of the things that no longer serve a purpose in our lives. Say bye-bye to those things and people who are toxic. It is time for you to unapologetically put yourself FIRST!

When you say that you won't have time for self-care, you are doubting the possibilities of you having time. You can have time if you make time. **How is it that we prioritize everything and everyone except for ourselves?** I think about how often many of us allow our phones to die. I know I'm guilty of letting my phone's battery get to 2% because I don't feel like getting up and putting it on the charger. Similarly, some of us will allow ourselves to become drained because we didn't feel like making time for ourselves. We didn't have time, because our schedules were so "busy." Why don't we have the time to engage in self-care?

We need to do an inventory on what consumes the bulk of our time. If we really take some time to reflect upon what and who is getting most of our time and commitment, we will be able to identify time for self-care. For me, I put my career before myself. I brought work home. Yes, it yielded favorable results, but it came at a cost. I felt drained. I felt like I was losing myself at times. I poured my heart and soul into my job and I was still denied the position I applied for. That experience left me feeling worthless. I began to doubt my worth. It hurt because others didn't see the value of my work like those who I interfaced with daily. I decided that I needed to take a mini me-cation to the beach for 3 days. During that time I reflected. I put my phone on 'do not disturb' and I refrained from checking e-mails. It was in the moment of peace that I realized I put too many eggs in one basket. I gave everything to my career and left nothing for myself.

I realized that I invested more in what made my supervisors happy. I focused on what made the company thrive, while I strive to survive. If I wasn't cautious I would've sold my mind, body, and soul in exchange for pay and benefits that I can't take with me when I leave this world. The hard truth is that **our positions are replaceable.**

Your Position is "Replaceable"

If you were to pass away, your job would replace you. Regardless of how great you are and how much of an impact you've made, your **position** is replaceable. Kevin O'Leary once said, "A salary is the drug they give you to forget your dream." Don't let that BE your reality. Don't forget your dream. When you clock out of work, clock into your dreams. It deserves the same, if not more energy than you give your job. In fact, work to BE your own boss! If your dreams do not scare you, you are not dreaming big enough. Think bigger! There is so much greatness in you, so do not downplay yourself by dreaming small. There is also too much greatness to sleep through your own dreams. Wake up and manifest it! Your position may be "replaceable," but your anointing, personality, talents, gifts, and perspectives can't be duplicated or replaced.

Sometimes we become so invested in our jobs that we neglect our primary job in life, which is to live. We often reach points amid life's conundrums, where we feel overwhelmed and stuck. We *feel* perplexed, stressed, overworked, exhausted, lost, invisible, and sometimes unappreciated. There are even times we *feel* like our backs are against the wall. We *feel* like we've done all we could do to overcome an issue, but the truth is we really haven't been open-minded about our issues.

When we are psychologically empty, we operate out of deficits, because there is nothing left to give. You cannot pour

into the lives of others with an empty cup. I've learned that the biggest goal should BE to BE in tune with our mind, body, and soul. We need to observe, reflect, learn from, and listen to ourselves. What is going on inside? Boats don't sink because of the water around the boat. Boats sink because the water on the outside of the boat got inside of the boat. Are you allowing the troubles of life on the outside to cause you to sink? DON'T! Grab your life jacket. Decree and declare that you will survive! You have tools at your disposal to survive! Use it!

We must make time for restoration! It has to be non-negotiable. You don't want to regret not maximizing the time to enjoy life when you **clock out** of this physical realm. Clock in some "me time," before the hospital clocks it in for you.

"Managing Stress"

Life has taught me to not focus solely on "managing stress." The concept of managing stress is like applying a band-aid to a wound. You should pay more attention to your stressors. Once we reflect on our stressors we can deal with the root of stress. Your stress at work may be decreased if you took a moment to reflect on how you deal with your stressors. For me, two major stressors were clients e-mailing me numerous questions and feeling overwhelmed by taking on too many tasks. I decided that we could do a better job at centralizing communication and essential documents for clients to access more easily. This decreased the amount of inquiries I received. I addressed the second stressor by learning to say "no" or to speak up when I need additional support. Sometimes we feel overwhelmed because we have too much on our plate. We have too much on our plate because **we**

allowed others to fill it. Pull back from the table! Take some things off your plate! We must work to address the root of stress by exploring ways to work through our stressors. A major stressor that many people grapple with is the proclivity to compare themselves to others. We invite multiple stressors, such as pressure and unrealistic expectations when we compare ourselves to others.

Comparison Kills

Comparison is a threat to your well-BEing. Yes, comparison can kill you! If we look at a dull pencil and a sharpened pencil, we will learn that looking sharp is effortless when one hasn't put in any work. Yes, people may look sharp, as if they have it all together, but sometimes those people are also struggling. That person may BE struggling with their identity or even a major life crisis. In fact, that person may BE wishing they were you! You never know. We have to govern our perceptions. People always say that everything that glitters isn't gold, but even if you don't glitter like gold, you should celebrate and appreciate your "dullness." It is your heart that will make you shine. Your sparkle should also radiate from the inside. Do not compare yourself to others.

Never forget that you were remarkably and uniquely crafted to BE the best! You cannot compete with another person's life. Life is not a competition. You do not know people's life story, struggles, insecurities, or the experiences that shaped them into who they are today. You don't know the tests behind their testimony or the story behind their glory! You don't know the price they paid to get to where they are. So, if you attempt to compare yourself to others, you have to also account for the blind spots of their lives. You have to account for the things that you don't see, and if you have that kind of time to account for others, you should reevaluate the quality of accounting you do for your own life. Comparison kills!

I've heard people make responses like, "That's like comparing apples to oranges," when they are in a debate. Every time I hear that statement I am reminded that you can't compare apples to apples either, because each apple is unique. Red, green, and golden apples all have different tastes. When you compare, you kill your uniqueness, your personal taste and everything that makes you great! Don't do it!

You couldn't BE me if you tried

If you walked in my shoes for one day, you'd rethink trying to compare yourself to me. When you wear my shoes, you wear my identity, beliefs, and you also experience my pain, my accountabilities, my struggles, and my realities. However, before you walk in my shoes, the shoes have to fit. Essentially, when we compare ourselves to others, we are forcing ourselves to fit into someone we are not! We are also forcing ourselves to fit into someone we think we know. Yes, it's ok to BE inspired by or to admire someone for their work, but don't relinquish your humanity in the process. Desire to BE a better version of yourself. The things that you appreciate about others should inspire you to do the things you need to do to develop those areas for growth in your life. If you appreciate how a person carries themselves, reflect upon what you need to do to enhance the way you carry yourself.

Contrary to popular belief, there is nothing wrong with asking a person you admire for feedback, advice, or how they got to where they are. Likewise, when people admire us, we should be willing to help and support them. You may love the way a person speaks and you desire to BE like them, but you don't know that they overcame a speech impediment to speak the way they do. You never know what people have endured to BE who they are! So, seek to BE a better you! We should also complement one another, but don't get too carried away with it. BE mindful that a complement isn't an indication that someone desires to pursue you.

Starve distractions. Feed your focus.

No matter what you do there will BE those who think you are their competition. Allow them to burn themselves out trying to compete with you. You must learn to starve distractions and feed your focus. You have bigger fish to fry, than to worry about their internal, fictitious competitions in their heads. Apply the energy you could give them towards manifesting your goals. I let people think they are competing with me, but in actuality they are competing with their perception of me. I want everyone to win. We all can BE great in our own way. Unfortunately they are competing with me. They are actually competing with my purpose and passion. My purpose drives who I am and what I do. If you compete with my purpose, you will lose. I don't say that in a spirit of arrogance. God is responsible for why I am here. If I'm living out my assignment, you can't compete with that because it's not yours. You have your own assignment. Complete that. Don't give any distraction the attention it longs for. Starve it by doing the things that feed your focus in a positive way

Investing in Self-Caring: Make Time

"I won't have time for self-care." Aht! Aht! Rephrase that. How can I make time for self-care? Overcome doubt by training your mind to create time. **You must see self-caring as an investment**. Identify your need to restore and make it a priority! For instance, experiencing tranquility is a major need of mine. I need time for peaceful, quiet, and still moments. It is through stillness that I am able to more clearly hear God speak through me. Stillness helps me to reflect and to gauge my overall wellness. It helps me to not BE moved by the world. Stillness helps me to hear my own self! In our fast-paced, technology-driven, and noisy world, it can BE so difficult to hear ourselves. Sometimes we underreact or overreact. It was in stillness that I was able to see how I've overreacted in some situations.

Catastrophizing is when we embody self-doubt by only envisioning the worst that could happen. Sometimes we spend too much time and energy thinking and working through problems that are non-existent. We consume our minds with "what ifs," exerting our natural human survival instinct preparing for the unexpected. Stop worrying about the troubles of tomorrow. You have no control over them. In certain situations, you have to cross the bridge when you get to it. However, you do need to develop and maintain a growth mindset to BE mentally prepared when you get to a bridge.

We tend to focus on "crossing the bridge" when in reality, we may be nowhere near a bridge. What I've learned is that some problems are best addressed in the moment. In fact, there are problems or challenges that you need to address currently, but you've neglected them by focusing on problems of the future. The psychological phenomenon of mental time traveling can BE a blessing and a curse. A blessing whereby we develop a sense of purpose and motivation to accomplish something in the future, but a curse when anxiety, worries, and doubts about the future distracts us from thinking, responding, and living in the present moment.

We can spend so much time and energy worrying about how we're going to get the down payment (in the future) that we delay opportunities in the present, to work on our credit score, become financially stable, and to deal with our current fiscal responsibilities. Problems of the future can seep into your overall mentality, because thoughts become actions. However, tranquility has helped me to see things in new ways as I focused on BEing in the moment. #keepcalm. I put my phone on 'do not disturb', I turn off my computer, I turn off my TV, I clear my schedule, and I just BE. Give yourself permission to "simply" BE.

Know Your Triggers

You will BE shot. It is inevitable. So, keep your bulletproof vest on. Put on your "full armor!" You have to BE conscientious of your emotional triggers by paying attention to who and what triggers you and why. I must admit, that naming triggers can BE difficult. There are also triggers that you are oblivious to or don't yet have the language to identify. However, we cannot ignore triggers. If we choose to ignore them, they will build up over time and explode when we least expect them. Like a can of soda, if we continue to shake the can, the pressure will build up and as soon as we open the top. There will BE an explosion. This is similar to triggers. Our mind is the can; the soda is our emotions; and the pressure building up are the triggers. The top of the can exploding represents our mouth and what comes out!

We must begin to seek the support of counselors, elders, and life coaches to identify our triggers and reflect upon how we respond to those triggers to become BETTER. People often talk about triggers, but neglect the conversation of what caused the trigger. A trigger is a response to pain. If we do not process and recover from pain, we will constantly BE shot with reminders of our pain. The reminders of our pain are triggers. Just as we have to attend firearm training to get our permit to learn how to shoot, we must also seek counseling to help us learn strategies to deal with pulled "triggers" so we can navigate through our pain. We have to learn resilient techniques to apply to recover.

What are your triggers?

Once you have identified your triggers and how you've responded to them, you need to establish boundaries. You cannot avoid triggers, but you can avoid who and what you allow to intentionally trigger you on a regular basis. Who do you talk to about your triggers? Who can you talk to about them? The hard reality is that we need to "unpack" our triggers. If we do not deal with our triggers now, they will be pulled later, resulting in the fatality of a relationship. Make a self-investment by scheduling a session with a licensed therapist or counselor. They will help you unpack your triggers and traumatic experiences in healthy and individually responsive ways. The first step is identifying your triggers. **You** have to do the work first. #BEaccountable.

Rethinking Healing in Isolation

Many of us feel that we heal best in isolation. We don't want to be bothered with the troubles of the world. We'd rather deal with our issues alone. We ignore texts, calls, and social events that cause us to interface with others. Sometimes we feel too embarrassed or ashamed to share with others what we're experiencing. Other times, we just don't trust many people with information about our personal lives. When you're trapped up in your own mess, that's all you have—your mess. Consequently, we become stuck in a place where we repeatedly hear and see the same messages that got us where we are in the first place. We hear the same voices in our head as we continue to beat ourselves up about our issues. Since we are alone, there is no one to intercede on our behalf. We continue to mope around, living in a bubble, and screaming through our minds for help, but no one sees or hears us. What if we forced ourselves out of bed and out of the house? We are able to inhale a breath of fresh air and connect with Mother Nature. We are able to hear the birds chirp and see the beauty of nature around us. Nature has a very unique and powerful healing capability. During times when you feel like isolating or closing yourself off from others, force yourself to remain connected to nature. It is clear that nature will speak to our hearts if we are mindful and grateful.

Even if you choose not to interact with others as you strive to self-heal, you should tune into inspirational podcasts or videos on YouTube. Simply search for motivational or inspirational songs, or pep talk videos and numerous videos will emerge. Force yourself to listen to those powerful messages. You need a counter-narrative to your narrative. You need someone to pour into you. You need to hear voices other than the ones in your head. Sometimes we don't know what words to pray, but if we truly believe in the power of God or a higher BEing, we know that He/She knows our hearts! All we need to do is to WALK by faith. Even when we do not see our healing, we need to WALK by faith! We need to MOVE! We need to keep ourselves active! We need to constantly feed ourselves positivity. We need to pray and meditate. When you don't know what to pray, just begin by BEing grateful (Chapter 1). Give thanks that you are still alive. Give thanks because you didn't lose your mind!

While you think you are alone and you enduring your healing journey in isolation, someone is praying for you! You never know what people are doing for you behind the scenes! Even if you do not feel like BEing bothered, you need to speak with a counselor. Although you should call on people who truly loves you, you need time and support in dealing with the root of the issues you are experiencing. Yes, your best friend can pick you up and take you on a weekend getaway, but if you do not deal with the root of your problems you'll return to your present state after the trip. This is why you need a licensed counselor to support you in navigating some of the internal work. Do it for you! You are worth it! Do not heal alone! There are tools out there to help you! Sometimes we may be looking at our situation through deficit lens or we may be overthinking.

We need to be prepared for transformation. A counseling session will help you identify the habits of mind and approaches to engage in a mental detox. You need to have efficient tools, approaches, and habits of mind, before you isolate yourself. We can spend too much time thinking deficit thoughts and misleading ourselves through destructive behaviors. Get help! Keep help! Normalize seeing your counselor or therapist regularly. Your friends are awesome, but not all of them are licensed to help you navigate your "stuff." Even if your best friend is a licensed counselor or therapist, sometimes we can benefit from having an outside perspective.

Rock bottom experiences can teach you lessons that mountain top experiences can't. You may fall, but don't stay there! Learn how to grip and catch yourself before you fall. Your mentors, elders, and counselors can help you find strategies to develop your ability to grip and catch yourself before you hit rock bottom. Rock bottom experiences can be learning experiences. Don't let rock bottom experiences be your norm.

Pass the courses of life. Don't repeat them.
There is a "teachable moment" in everything.

BE Unbothered By People

You must BE unapologetically self-caring. I've had people close to me, both personally and professionally tell me to my face that I wasn't "doing enough." Although from my perspective, I poured out my heart and soul, it was still not "good enough" for others. Hearing their perception of my giving as insufficient was like a dagger to my heart. It almost broke me. Then, I realized that their perception of my giving was based on how they perceived my strength, rather than my weaknesses. To some, I could be perceived as a human bank, with endless money to give. I give what I can, but I could give more. This is based on a person's perception of your finances. Yes, it's none of their business, but unfortunately many people see your glory, but they don't know your priorities. They see your income streams, but they don't know what it takes to fund your dreams behind the scenes. There are those that feel they are entitled to your harvest, although they didn't sow. They don't understand the level of sacrifice it took for you to have your harvest. While many were out partying and living their best life, I was making investments in myself by reading, writing, and working on my dissertation. Yes, I earned a doctorate by the age of 30, but it came with a cost! Yes, I serve on several boards and hold several leadership positions, but it came with a cost! I lost my "freedom" to truly be "free" in public. I have to consider what I post on social media. I have to consider who I'm with and what I wear, say, and do while I'm in public. Some may see my behavior as "acting brand new," because I am a brand. People want to profit and benefit from your brand, but aren't willing to appreciate your sacrifices to get to that point or contribute towards your dream. People see your job promotion and all they visualize is dollar signs. They don't know what you're about to endure for a salary increase, that can't compensate you for the turbulence you're about to experience, because of your elevation. They will still say you can and should do more, although they don't know what it's like to walk in your shoes, while carrying a full plate with sides, deserts, and a to-go order. They don't know about the late nights you spent off the clock developing and perfecting projects for work. They see strength and power although you wake up countless mornings praying for the strength and power to even make it out of bed! You portray a powerful image, but you're running on "E." You're everyone's superhero; but who will save you? I've said all of that to say, when you've given it your all, there will still be those who've never step backstage, who will say to your face, "It's not good enough." If you listen to them, you will murder your own potential. You will go to trial for your own tribulations. You will be sentenced for your response to the sentence they spoke to you. You've already been sentenced to life in the prison of social norms, expectations, religion, and social acceptance. If you try to escape or resist the prison, there will be a price to pay. What I do know for sure is that you should never allow the opinions, beliefs, wants, and perceptions of others to dictate how you choose to BE! If you give all, you won't have anything left for yourself! People want their cake and eat it, share it, and sell it too. BE self-caring! Don't allow anyone to make you feel guilty for not doing what they want you to do, because they don't know what it's like to BE you. They must wear your shoes; bear your burdens; experience your pain; endure your struggles; and embrace your past to BE in a position to tell you what you should do with the time and energy that God has planted within you. Some of the people who will assassinate you with their words and expectations, will be the same ones weeping the loudest at your funeral. Resist, reflect, recuperate , restore, and reclaim your time! I now know what my cousin, Bishop Dr. Eric Hall meant when he said he was "so glad that God delivered him from people". People are not your God. BE unapologetically self-caring!

Establish Your Hedge of Protection—Your Boundaries

Identify and proclaim what you will not tolerate. Make up in your mind what your boundaries will BE and **BE Consistent** (see Chapter 6). You must put your foot down and stand your ground to maintain your boundaries. You must communicate your boundaries to others, so they will BE aware of how to handle you. Sometimes you have to teach people how to treat you. People who genuinely care about you will respect your boundaries. When people do not respect my boundaries, I have to let them know, "What you not gone' do is" is disrespect me, my time, or my space. This is non-negotiable. If you allow people to disrespect you, your time, and your space, you are doing yourself a disservice. No, I'm not recommending that you should physically fight someone, but you should ensure that they understand that you are *not the one.* BLOCK people if necessary.

Although there is a hedge of protection around you and you should have no **doubts**, you must BE confident in who you are and the power invested in you to SPEAK cancellation to any negative or evil forces that come up against you! You must SPEAK victory during the battle. "When the enemy comes in like a flood, the Spirit of the Lord will lift up a standard against him and put him to fight" (Isaiah 59:19). What I now know for sure is that although the Spirit of the Lord lifts up a standard, you need to do your part in maintaining those STANDARDS. We have to remain steadfast and unmovable in sustaining our standards/boundaries.

Remember, we must BE open-minded, so although you may not agree to the source (i.e., biblical scriptures, Buddha), we can appreciate the perspective it can provide for our edification. We've explored why we should invest in self-love, so what we not gone' do is entertain fake love.

No Time for Fake Love

I've been down so long it look like up to me. They look up to me. I got fake people showin' fake love to me. Straight up to my face, straight up to my face. I've been down so long it look like up to me. They look up to me. I got fake people showin' fake love to me......Whole time they wanna take my place.

-Drake, Fake Love (2017)

I was sitting in a keynote presentation given by my academic sister Dr. Dywanna Smith and she spoke the words of 1993 Nobel Prize winner for literature, Toni Morrison, "Love is or it ain't. Thin love ain't love at all." At that moment, my life paused for five seconds as I dealt with the stark reminder of all the times I fell for the 'thin' love people dished at me. I fell for the superficial love—that "fake love" as rapper, singer, songwriter, actor, producer, and entrepreneur Drake calls it. People will say they love you, but lack the capacity to even love you at your fullest expression. They don't have the capacity to love you. They can only take and handle parts of you. Some of them only love access to you.

While there are those people who love the hell out of you, there are those who love the hell in you. They will suffocate the gift in you and strangle you to "death" with their toxic words, slick shade, condescending expressions, secret eye rolls, and silent, strategic plots to manifest you as their company in their mansion of misery. Before you know it, your goals and your dares to dream becomes determinations of doubt. You begin to doubt who you are, slipping into a state of depression, wondering, how did I get here? Unbeknownst to you, those who you thought "loved" you were fraudulent. They were able to package "love" in a way they knew would appeal to you.

Fake lovers and "friendemies" are very studious, intelligent, and meticulous. Because they secretly love the concept of you while simultaneously despising the 'you' they wish they were, they spend a considerable amount of time studying who they think you are. Consequently, these fraudulent lovers or fans in denial plot against you like thieves in the middle of the night. They know when you're most vulnerable, because you posted about it (They didn't click like, by the way). They know when you're not home, because you posted about it. They know what you're about to do, because you posted about it. That's your problem. Stop posting your every move and plan. How can you be upset with your enemies when you gave them the blueprint to ambush your plans? **Work in silence, let your success make the noise, because I've learned that prematurely posting your plans can prevent production.** If you build in silence, they wouldn't know where to attack, what to attack, and when to attack!

Your friendemies have shown you fake love when you've invited them over to your house. They've made comments like, "Mmm, must BE nice." They complemented you on your success and then instantly injected themselves within the compliment, "I mean, I would've gotten my doctorate, but I just don't want any more student loans." "Nice, house. I'm so glad I don't have to worry about cutting the grass at my apartment." "I would've gotten a house, but I don't have time to pay the H.O.A." They will show you fake love, and we will still love them long enough for them to break in and rob our time, our energy, and our joy; because we gave them the access to do so.

We were vulnerable and allowed those backstabbers into our physical and mental spaces "to smile in our faces and the whole time they wanna' take our place," as the O'Jays sang. We thought they were friends and family because we were focused more on who we thought they were, but the O'Jays reminds us that we need to focus more on "what they do." Someone is mad because you chose peace over drama and distance over disrespect. They will BE alright! In the words of my sister, Anastashia Broughton, "People change, money don't." Focus on stacking your money and BEing a better you.

Love is a noun, a verb, and in some cases, an adjective. Dr. Toni Morrison cautioned us, love is or it ain't. There is no such thing as fake love. 1 Corinthians 13, verses 4 through 8 in the New International Version states, "Love is patient, love is kind. It does not envy, it does not boast, it is not proud. It does not dishonor others, it is not self-seeking, it is not easily angered, it keeps no record of wrongs. Love does not delight in evil but rejoices with the truth. **It always protects**, always trusts, always hopes, always perseveres. Love never fails."

Love Always Protects

In my preacher's voice, "I don't know who needs to hear this, but love always protects!" If people truly love you, they will protect you. They will BE your ram in the bush. These are the people who will call you out. They will tell you about the booger you have in your nose, when others will allow you to walk around all day with it hanging. They will call you like my friends, Queen-Tribling and Antoine Deas, and tell you, "Um, add a comma and delete that extra 'o' in your Facebook status, NOW!" These people are like guardian angels in the flesh. They will do everything in their power to ensure you are successful. They can also sense when you are about to BE burned out or when you are struggling. Rather than talk about it, these people show up! They will pull up on you and kidnap you (in a good way) to get you to snap out of whatever you are going through. They will listen to your issue to understand what's going on, so they can best support you. If they can't provide you the support you need, they will only refer you to a person they trust. They possess that thick love! I've learned that these are the people you should cherish and reciprocate thick love to. However, there will BE times when the love they demonstrate hurts. They will tell you about yourself and mandate that you get yourself together. These people will love the hell out of you! Call them. Check up on them. Love on them back!

The Board

I have created a board of trustees in my life that encompasses mentors and friends who have the capacity to serve as mentors. These are the people I go to for advice because they **know** and love me. They have **demonstrated** a positive impact through their life's work. I surround myself with people who possess the character and have demonstrated integrity in different roles. Typically, a board of trustees is responsible for ensuring that a school or organization is operating in ways that fulfill and advance the school's mission. The board usually works to establish and approve policies, strategic goals, and objectives.

Similarly, I have a board of trustees who supports me in fulfilling my mission in life, by loving and supporting me with policies, strategic goals, and objectives. These "board members" are aware that they are my mentors, but they have no clue they are serving on a "board" because the board part is mental for me. My mother and father also serves on the board. When it comes to mechanics or anything handy, my father is my go to. One phone call to him and I will be able to troubleshoot the problem.

As custom with a typical board, I usually present my idea or situation to each board member for them to "review" for feedback. This submission could occur through phone conversations, over lunch/brunch/dinner, or even through a direct message on social media. I force myself to remain open when anticipating their responses, because I know they are responding out of love. After receiving feedback from all board members, I begin to think through their feedback and weigh my options. When I have questions after I've done my homework, I return to my board members with follow-up questions. Their various perspectives are very enlightening, which supports me in making sound decisions. They love me enough to ensure I outweigh all of my options before making my move. I trust their feedback because they **love** me.

Board Criteria: No Title Bearers Allowed

There are people who have had the titles, the positions, and the ideal careers; but lack the ability to demonstrate a positive impact in those capacities. What good is it to have a title without yielding positive results? Many of us have or know of some people who have an infatuation with titles. I am DR...I am State Director...I am Head Supervisor. These "leaders" are so caught up in their titles that they become entangled in unproductivity. In fact, these "leaders" are productive because they are typically being productive in occupying their title. They are passionate about their title and not their tasks as leaders. They are passionate about being called by their title, but they refuse to answer their calling. They bear the title, but bear no fruit. When asked, "Who are you?", they often reply with their titles. "A title is only important if one's character and integrity dictates its use" (Call Me MISTER vision statement). Many people have the title, but lack the character, the integrity, the respect, the valor, and the capacity to efficiently execute the deliverables they've been called to manifest. They may have the credentials, but can't apply theory and knowledge to practice. They have a suit, but aren't best suited for the position. Why not? Their character truly makes them who they are. Your title indicates the role you perform on and for a team. Many "leaders" are often embellished with credentials, but who are they when the storms of life come raging in the workplace? BE careful who you follow. Their true character and motive always reveals itself under pressure.

I know you're probably thinking, how did I get my mentors? The quick answer is some I reached out and asked them to BE my mentor. Others, came naturally. However, I had to **allow** them to love me. **Don't ask people to mentor you if you are not willing to listen and learn from them.** Some people desire to get love, but not to BE loved. They are often caught up in the happy feelings associated with love, but when love begins to protect, by any means necessary, they resist it. As I've shared before, sometimes those who love you will share insight that may trigger for you. They may tell you that you need to clean up your social media or that the person you are dating is toxic for you, which causes you to grapple with many emotions and decisions. In these moments, I have found time and reflection to BE the best healers.

I remember getting feedback from my dissertation chair on my writing. I just knew that I was amongst the best scholars in the program, and when I opened up that word document and saw all of those red comments, I nearly fainted. When I received her e-mails regarding corrections to my work, it took me 24 hours to process the feedback alone. Notice I used feedback and not criticism. It took time to deal with the areas my academic mentor identified as areas for improvement. The best part of her feedback was that it was **heavy on the thick love.** Out of love, her feedback also provided suggestions for me to consider which supported me in refining my writing. Again, these are the type of people you have to remain connected to, but you have to BE willing to **BE loved**. That is, BEing open to the multiple ways of loving even when it "hurts." It is through the temporary pain that love can cause us to learn that pressure produces products. Pearls are made under pressure. Pearls also represent wisdom. Allow the pressures of your process to produce pearls (wisdom) you need to apply in your process of BEing better.

Building your self-caring arsenal

Self-caring is a multidimensional, multifaceted process of intentionally **deciding** to do the things that are necessary to cultivate our overall wellness. There are numerous dimensions to engaging in self-care. I will share some information to help you build your personal self-care arsenal. You should seek a certified counselor and a life coach for additional support. This portion will help you get started! Take what you need and BE affirmed if you already have some of these ideas or concepts in your arsenal:

Personal (Spiritual, Emotional, Intellectual)

Invest time in:

- things that stimulate your endorphins (Happy hormones)
- "ME time"
  Stop! Plan and book your ME-cation now! Don't worry about the cost, just go! One day, I woke up, shoved my beach towel, sunscreen, beach chair, beach umbrella, and necessities in the car and traveled to the beach. I purchased clothes when I got there. Sometimes you need to get away without being critical or too analytical. Don't let finances BE a limitation. Just go! It's perfectly ok to just do NOTHING! It's ok to simply go to BE in the moment. We can do great spiritual work and self-healing

when we establish uninterrupted time to just BE. Do not check your e-mails or engage in anything work related. You deserve this time for yourself. People will ask why you didn't invite them. Just inform them that you needed some "Me time." If they feel offended or become upset with you....they will BE alright. I'm sure they'd rather have the opportunity to BE upset with you than to mourn you, because you didn't take care of yourself. Get over them and into you! YOU NEED AND DESERVE YOUR PEACE! Sometimes you have to "fast" from people.

- journaling
- focusing on what's going right
- establishing and maintaining boundaries
- doing what you love
- treating yourself (don't worry about counting calories)
- reading a great book
- reflection
- prayer
- meditation
- engaging with nature
- getting a breath of fresh air
- doing something you've never done before
- into activities that you find relaxing
- in developing your social-emotional skills
- taking a break when necessary

Social

Invest time
- connecting with people who love you
- in reaching out to check in on friends
- making calls even when you think you're a bother
- in sustaining friendships by making quality time
- asking for support
- establishing and maintaining deliberate hedges of protections.
- Identifying your needs, beliefs, wants, standards (expectations), and non-negotiables; and BE consistent with them

Environmental

Invest in:

- establishing and maintaining spaces that make you happy. Put time into your home and work setting décor. Your space is a sanctuary. I take my environments seriously
- clean and safe environments
- clutter-free environments. A cluttered physical space can cultivate a cluttered mental space. Flowing energy is essential to your mental space. Study up on Fung Shei. It is very enlightening

Physical

Invest time in:

- eating. If I do not eat, I get hangry! I make time to eat because food fuels my energy. I've also made a conscious effort not to have a working breakfast, lunch, or dinner. I take the time to devote 100% attention to enjoying my food. STOP and disconnect to enjoy your food
- staying hydrated
- 7-8 hours of sleep
- consistent exercise. Movement stimulates oxygen throughout your body and boosts your immune system
- stretching
- walking or hiking
- yoga
- dancing. I have generated a playlist of music that makes me happy and gets me moving
- maintaining a healthy diet. Meal prep if you need to
- getting physicals
- enjoying kisses from the sun! Sunlight provides vitamin D

Financial

Invest time in

- saving money
- budgeting and sticking to it
- engaging in financial literacy development. I've learned a lot from credible YouTube videos and people on Clubhouse. BE careful who you listen to. Make sure the sources are credible
- signing up for and attend financial literacy courses or workshops (i.e., learn about credit, interest rates, etc.)
- considering multiple streams of income when necessary
- managing and documenting your finances
- learning about stocks
- paying back people you owe. If you are reading this and you owe me money, **run me my coins**. I don't care how rich I get, I still need my money. People work hard for their money. Show them respect for their hard-earned money and return it in a timely fashion.

Technological

Invest time in:

- unplugging when necessary and don't feel the need to announce it to the world.
- establishing and maintain social media boundaries. If you don't want people in your business, don't post about it
- maintaining your brand on social media
- using technology to your advantage to access new knowledge and learn new skills

Add your own here:

Professional

Invest time in:

- engaging in time blocking
- establishing work boundaries
- BEing mindful of adding certain co-workers to social media
- taking breaks
- taking a mental health day if needed
- putting your health first
- documenting everything
- refraining from multi-tasking. Multi-tasking is a myth. Scientifically your brain can only focus on one specific task at a time. Do the job right the first time. Delegate and ask for help when necessary.
- stressing out about managing time. You cannot manage time. You are not God. You do not control time. You manipulate your time by blocking out time to take care of certain matters. This is a hard reality because my schedule never goes as planned. I stopped using a physical planner because of this. I plug everything into my phone. Consciously engage in time blocking. People make time for what they want. (Don't debate me)
- registering for professional development that interests you. Do not wait for someone to mandate professional development. You should attend workshops and conferences to better yourself. You should get something out of the deal. Do this for you, not your job.
- reflecting and eliciting feedback
- When you get a performance evaluation, do not beat yourself up. This is an opportunity to learn about possible blind spots. Listen and ask questions. I've also learned to ask for specific recommendations. It's easy to BE critiqued, but those who evaluate you should also BE willing to provide specific feedback. In the interim, always remember to reflect upon if what you are doing aligns with your personal mission and the mission of the company/organization

MY SELF-CARE GOALS

Create a list of self-care goals. This is all about what you! It is time for you to treat yourself! Plan that trip! Prioritize yourself!

CHAPTER 6

BE CONSISTENT
with discernment

BE CONSISTENT

"We are what we repeatedly do. Excellence,
then, is not an act, but a habit."
–Aristotle

Affirmation: I will overcome doubting my ability to BE. I will remain consistent in manifesting my goals and dreams.

T hought is the architect and repeated action is the builder. To BE consistent, you have to starve your distractions and feed your focus. If you continue to feed a stray cat, the cat will continue returning to eat. Eventually, like distractions, the cat will reside where your attention resides. I created a 4E Plan which encompasses a cyclical process of enforcing, and educating to remain consistent in manifesting my goals.

Your vision and ideas (the blueprint) will remain a construction site until you generate a plan and a committed team to consistently manifest your ideas. Distractions are inevitable. We make the choice of whether or not we give distractions power. To BE steadfast means to BE firm and unmovable, in spite of adversity. I've learned that BEing steadfast requires that you embrace everything you are accountable for. If you want a chiseled body, you have to embrace everything that comes with manifesting that goal into a reality. You have to BE accountable for and to your goals by embracing the mindset that is consistent with your goals. You can desire to lose a few pounds, but if you have a fast food mentality your bed is going to BE the only thing losing pounds the moment you lift up off of it. Therefore, you must envision everything that you do as an investment towards making your dreams a reality.

Your goals don't care about how you feel. Each thought you embrace funds the work towards BEing a better you. If you want a consistent paycheck you must embrace your responsibility to put your time in to be compensated. No work. No paycheck. No consistent work. No consistent paycheck.

Step 1: Embrace

Embrace a "by any means necessary" mentality. This mentality encompasses an attitude that refrains from making any excuses. **Excuses are rendered by people who take opportunity for granted.** Someone took the same cards you were dealt and played them, because they wanted something bad enough. You'll make time if you value it. You'll do what it takes if you want it bad enough. Let's face it. You're always going to have a busy schedule. So, if you don't get beyond the excuses, your busy schedule will always impede your progress. I had to force myself to embrace new, more productive and healthier habits. I had to block out time to engage in new habits that aligned with my goals. I've learned that investing some time is better than no time. So, if I go to the gym and only spend 15 minutes, it's better than not going at all. **Slow progress is still progress; and don't allow anyone to tell you differently.** We must condition our minds to empower ourselves to manifest our goals, regardless of how we feel. Instead of telling people not to procrastinate, I always encourage them to procrastinate, **because I believe procrastination is the best teacher. It will teach** you why you shouldn't procrastinate during the most inconvenient times. Some people have to learn the hard way. So, get started, because not getting started is time wasted.

Step 2: Empower

Words have enormous power. The God in you is activated by the words you speak. From the beginning of time, words have been used in powerful ways, such as, to manifest things. Let there BE light, and there was light! Thus, you have been given authority to empower yourself, to empower ideas, and to inspire others. You can't expect others to cheer for you if you don't cheer for yourself. We have to BE our own cheerleaders! I was taught as a young child that I had to BELIEVE in myself. Life has taught me that believing in myself is easier when I understand who and what I'm believing in.

Your potential is your greatest investment.

Greater is He/She that is in you! Yes, I don't believe in limiting who God is. You are filled with enormous and uncalculatable potential. You have a purpose here on Earth. Otherwise, why were you created? Part of your purpose is to CREATE—to manifest! When you rise in the morning, you may not feel like getting up out of bed, but you must force yourself to get up. Scientifically, your brain **sends commands** to your extremities. Your body responds to the commands and responds by driving you out of bed. Your commands ignited actions. Likewise, you must command yourself to BE consistent. You must BE your own inner coach. Talk to yourself! Push yourself! You must blow the whistle and call yourself out! You must demand the best from yourself! You must know the plays and you must play them! You must never forget the power that has been invested in you to empower yourself! You must command your mind, your mouth, and your body to manifest during each moment of your mission in life.

Consistency is not always convenient. If you say you're going to do it, you have to do it consistently. Yes, you will BE tempted. It's inevitable. Yes, you will have moments when you will veer off track, but you have to redirect your actions with affirmations to command your body to realign with your goals. I WILL NOT STOP AT KRISPY KREME DOUGHNUTS! I WILL NOT BE TEMPTED BY THIS RED HOT SIGN! I HAVE ABS TO GET BY THE SUMMER!

Ok, well, maybe I'll just eat one doughnut? I purchased one doughnut and what happened? I began to crave more! One moment of inconsistency is an invitation to make excuses to BE inconsistent. Recite your affirmations and command your mind and body to stick to your goals. I write post-it notes with affirmations and post them everywhere. I make a conscious effort to read them, because otherwise they will BEcome just a piece of paper on the wall. I also set reminders on my phone with affirmations and goals. I get to the point where I also put inspirational quotes and images that remind me of my goals on my phone and computer wallpapers. Feed your subconscious with visual reminders. You should also get an accountability partner, who you should also support on their journey.

Stick To Your Proven Recipe

You have the recipe and it works! You've been producing the best pound cake in the world, because you've been sticking to the measurements. You've been consistent using specific items that make your cake great. However, you begin to slack up on your measurements, putting a little too much or a little too less here and there. You begin to slack up on specific items, omitting various items that are essential to your recipe. You begin substituting one item for the next. You even begin to add new items to your recipe in hopes of it producing consistent results.

Thanksgiving is here and everyone is ecstatic about trying your famous pound cake. Everyone says, "It's good" and "It's tasty." However, for the first time ever, you have leftovers remaining. In fact, half of the cake remained untouched. What happened? You fell prey to inconsistency. You took for granted the power of your recipe—the formula that produced consistent results. Like that cake, when you slack up on your measurements, putting a little too much time here on unproductive things and a little too less time here on productive things, you don't yield the results you desire. You don't yield the results you desire when you slack up on the specific items like your studying, working out, getting adequate sleep, taking mental breaks, meditation/prayer, affirmations, and planning, amid other things that you know work. Why? You failed to empower yourself to stick to the recipe that has consistently provided favorable results. You can always throw a cake in the trash and bake another, but you should not take a risk on your reputation, potential, or time. It's too important. Put power into the things and thoughts that will empower you to manifest your goals.

Step 3: Enforce

It is time to apply that pressure! True power comes when you begin to enforce and reinforce your goals. You must execute and engage in healthy habits that are consistent with your goals, even if it requires additional pressure. Olives produce oil under pressure. Toothpaste is extracted under pressure. Popcorns are produced under pressure. Diamonds and wine are produced under pressure. Car movement is produced under the pressure. However, many of us tend to apply pressure or energy into everything except for what we should BE applying pressure towards. Just because you're applying pressure doesn't mean you will yield awesome results. What are you producing under pressure? Sometimes we apply the wrong pressure on the wrong things.

The same energy we channel towards chasing behind people is the same energy we should use to chase our dreams. The same energy we channel towards posting on social media is the same energy we're 'post' (supposed) to BE channeling towards our goals. The same energy we use worrying and doubting, is the same energy we should channel towards believing and investing in ourselves. Keep that same energy to encourage yourself.

BE a warrior, not a worrier!

You can embrace your calling and empower yourself all you want, but **nothing happens until you enforce and reinforce it.** A shift begins to happen when you begin to enforce the actions that will make your dreams a reality. You must BE vigilant of people who interrupt what you enforce. There are people who will distract you as you are applying the pressure necessary to BE a better you. Many of these people want the pressure you're applying on your goal applied to their goals and interests instead. Before you know it, you'll BE fueling energy to enforce the things that make them happy as you neglect yours dreams. You'll end up using your blueprint to build their dream. Don't do it!

Step 4: Educate

We discussed earlier that a **_real education_** is the process of BEing a better you. This encompasses taking advantage of teaching and learning experiences that edify your mind, body, and soul. You can to learn through and from your experiences if you are attentive and reflective. I call these "teachable moments." Education is essential to BEing and remaining consistent. The process of researching, studying, and analyzing your thoughts, behavior patterns, and the behaviors of others will help you learn about yourself. This self-discovery is essential, because you can lose yourself if you are mis-educated. You'll believe anything that anyone tells you. If you hang around the wrong people too long, they'll have you doubting everything about yourself. You could have earned a doctorate, but the wrong people will have you questioning why you pursued it in the first place.

The process of education helps to keep you grounded in remembering who you are, what you are about, what your calling is, why your calling is so essential, why you do what you do, and what you need to do to continue rising towards greatness. I've learned that when I apply education to my personal life, I am able to R.I.S.E. above adversity in the following ways: R-REFLECT, I-INTROSPECT, S-STRATEGIZE, and E-EXECUTE. When you learn better, you should choose to BE better. Some people know better and choose not to BE better.

BE Loyal

If you love and support someone, BE consistent in your love and support to them. What goes around comes around and what you put out will come back to you. Disloyalty can tarnish personal and professional relationships. Loyalty is not always convenient. Your loyalty should BE consistent when times are good and bad. Your loyalty should BE unconditional. Either you're loyal or you're not. If you're going to have my back, always have my back. If you are in a conversation with someone you're cool with and they drag my name through the mud, will you *still* have my back? You may not agree with my actions, but will you *allow* the person to speak negatively about me?

Like love, there's no in-between. If you say you're going to BE loyal to our organization, will you leave when things get rough? Will you leave when we don't see eye to eye? Is it easy for you to just walk out, if you are loyal? If so, then you have to BE mindful of what you commit yourself to in the first place. Perhaps, you should refrain from granting someone or something your loyalty too soon. Trust and respect must

BE earned over time. You have to build trust through the **consistent** demonstrations of trustworthiness. Trust cannot exist in the absence of **consistent** honesty. We have all been lied to before. All it takes is one lie to threaten trust.

So, How Can I Remain Consistent?

Webster's Diction defines consistency as an "agreement or harmony of parts or features to one another or a whole: Correspondence." Are your actions aligned with your values, goals, and purpose? Do you practice what you preach? What we believe must work in harmony or agreement with our actions. Numerous motivational speakers, coaches, and especially fitness trainers emphasize the essence of consistency. They contend that if you are consistent, you will witness results. I agree—somewhat.

Simply BEing consistent is insufficient. You can consistently make poor decisions. You can consistently eat burgers and fries and consistently have high cholesterol. You can consistently maintain White supremacy and disenfranchise people who have been consistently marginalized and oppressed. You can consistently BE inconsistent in doing the things necessary for you to produce favorable outcomes. Consistency must BE driven by discernment. One must **BE conscious** of what they're consistent in and if their consistency is consistent with what they truly believe.

We live in a microwave society where people expect instant results. People expect a harvest by watering the soil occasionally. People expect to unveil a banging body after one week in the gym. Some students expect to earn a 4.0 after one semester of consistently submitting quality work. While instantaneous results provide instant gratification, many people become disappointed when things return back to their previous state. They are disappointed when they gain the weight back. They are disappointed when their GPA drops back down to a 3.0. This can occur if we become consistent in the wrong things. **Persistence will help you acquire it, but consistency with discernment will help you sustain it.**

- Remember your why
- Set realistic and specific objectives
- Demolish doubt & think positively
- Call yourself out when you make excuses: Make time
- Do the small things well. Start small. Going for 5 mins is better than not going
- Celebrate the small wins
- Set reminders and track your habits
- Get an accountability partner
- Post and read affirmations
- Listen to affirmative and positive messages

Create a manifestation board

I have a wall devoted to my vision. Typically people create vision boards, but I found that I need something tangible. It's one thing to envision and another thing to actually manifest your goals. I use large sticky chart paper to lay out my visions. I place major goals under key headings: personal, professional, business, and family/friends. Under those headings I list personal, professional, business, and other goals with steps I need to take to achieve them. I attach the goals of my family members and friends under 'other,' so that I can support them in envisioning and manifesting their goals. We have to support each other. I attach deadlines to some of the small steps on my chart. I take a picture of my charts and I convert them into a wallpaper on my phone. I store them on my phone as a reference. I also use a checklist/reminder app that aligns with the goals on my wall. This is one approach I use to hold myself accountable. I do not share my vision with everyone. In fact, I do not let people I do not trust into my home.

4 Things I've learned:
Never post everything you think
Never post everything you're going through.
Never always post you whereabouts.
Never post your plans.

Opportunities and enemies are watching!

CHAPTER 7

BE P.E.T.T.Y.

BE P.E.T.T.Y.

"There is no real doing in the world without being first. Being, your presence, your connection to yourself and that which is greater than yourself, is far more important than what you do, but also is the thing that fuels what you do"-Oprah Winfrey

Affirmation: I will overcome doubting that I can acquire what I desire. I will overcome doubting myself. My values, perspectives, truths, experiences, preferences, desires, needs, beliefs, and life matters.

According to Merriam-Webster dictionary, petty means "having secondary rank or importance: minor; having little or no importance or significance; or marked by or reflective of narrow interests and sympathies: small-minded." The urban dictionary goes on to describe being petty as making a "big deal" over something "small." What you perceive as petty may actually be an observation that warrants attention. I didn't realize that much of what others and I perceived as "petty" was cloaked as accountability. However, what I know for sure is that small things do make a significant impact.

99 and A Half Won't Do

Petty cash is a small amount of money that is typically on hand. Rather than writing someone a check for five dollars, you can just pay them five dollars from the *petty* cash. For instance, five thousand dollars is a significant amount of money, so it would not be deemed suitable for the petty cash. Many people won't make petty cash a big deal because it's just a 'little' change. However, if your organization's goal was to raise $1,000 for the fundraiser and you all achieved the $975 mark, the petty cash all of a sudden becomes *essential*. You all need that 'little' $25 to meet your goal. Again, small things can make a big impact. After all, if you're trying to make $100, 99 and a half won't do! **Small things can make a significant impact.**

Pay Attention to Details

I always taught my students to pay attention to details. A fond memory of teaching the life lesson of paying attention to details occurred in my first grade class. After two days of teaching my students about lines, line segments, and rays, I asked my students to "line up," because we were heading to outdoor play. One student raised her hand. She said, "Mr.B, it's actually a line segment, because we have two ending points. The line leader is at the beginning. Sarah is at the end of the line. That makes this a line segment." My first grader checked me! Although I felt some type of way, I replied, "Yes, you're correct. I should've asked you all to form a line segment instead." (Now run me my line segment, I thought).

The first teachable moment was that we are all eternal learners who must acknowledge that we are not always right. We must BE teachable. The second teachable moment is that small things can make a big impact. I could've said, "Now that's petty" to my student, but a line and a line segment are not synonymous. People tend to call you petty for highlighting things that need to BE corrected. I firmly believe that the term petty can BE used as a deflection mechanism. That is, people will call you petty to avoid dealing with an issue because it's a "little" issue to them, although it is a relevant issue to you. It's not petty; it's accountability. **Small things can make a significant impact. #BEP.E.T.T.Y.**

SMALL In A Significant Way

My favorite color is Caribbean Blue—not turquoise, aqua, teal, blue, or green. It's Caribbean Blue. If the wedding colors are Caribbean Blue, gold, and champagne and some members of the bridal party wore turquoise, it would make a big difference to me! You may not notice the difference, and you may even feel that I'm making a big deal out of 'nothing.' However, as an artist, the exact colors are essential to me.

We have graphic identity colors to ensure we are using the exact color. Interior designers, graphic designers, wedding planners, architects, fashion designers, painters, and anyone with an artistic eye all understand my point. Members of fraternities and sororities can also agree that exact colors *matter*. My fraternity's colors are old gold and black—not gold, yellow, marigold, or bronze. It's old gold and black—respect that. It's Alpha Phi Alpha, not Affa Phi Affa. **Small things can make a significant impact. It's okay to #BEP.E.T.T.Y.**

It's How You Use it

People say I'm petty and in some instances, I am—but in a constructive, humorous way. However, there are people who are petty in shady, destructive, and vindictive ways. These people amplify "small" things as an attempt to destroy your spirit, image, and reputation. I've learned that words can BE manipulated to have positive or negative connotations. When someone says, "You killed that," they are referring to a person executing something with a spirit of excellence. They are not referring to murder. When someone says, "She was bad," they are not referring to her BEing a bad person. Bad is used in a positive manner to highlight how good she looked. So, it's not solely about what you do, but how you do it. It's not solely about what you say, but how you say it. It's not solely about being petty, but how and why you do it. **Small things can make a significant impact.**

It's the Small Things, For Me

It's the small wins that lead to the big win! It's the small habits that shape consistency. It's the small deposits that lead to the big payoff! It's the small beliefs that lead to the big dream! As I've intentionally restated, small things can make a significant impact. Although, those small things may be insignificant to you, always be open to the notion that everyone is entitled to their own truth. You can become overwhelmed striving to overtake goals that seem insurmountable. In those instances, you may learn that it's the removal of those small stones that will make a grand impact on your progress towards your goal.

> **"The man who moves a mountain begins by carrying away small stones". – Confucius.**

Every action we take, whether big or small has an impact. Thus, we must be conscious of what we entertain. Even a little entertainment can make a significant impact. If you give a clown a circus, it will perform! If you record them, they will perform. If you feed it, it will eat. If you pay it, it will take. If you follow it, it will lead. If you eat it, it will digest. If you say it, you will become it. If you write it, it will manifest. If you entertain the thought of BEing better, you will purposefully channel your time, energy and passion towards BEing better. We must celebrate the small wins and recognize the significance of doing small things well to yield big results. Thus, I've learned that in order to BE better iterations of ourselves, we must BE P.E.T.T.Y.: **p**-urposefully **e**-ntertaining **t**-hose **t**-hings **y**-ou desire.

CHAPTER 8

BE IMPACTFUL

BE IMPACTFUL

> *"If you ever doubt your ability to make an impact or believe that you're too small to have an impact, remember the impact a mosquito had on you"*
>
> –Anthony Broughton

Affirmation: I will overcome doubting my ability to make a positive impact.

tiny mosquito can make a big impact on you! You felt the bite and hours later, you still feel it. No matter how small you are, never underestimate the magnitude of your impact. When I think of the work of Cicely Tyson, I think of how impactful she was. BEing busy and productive are not always effective. Sometimes we are busy in unproductive ways, because we have not committed to self-care. You can produce and still not BE impactful in a positive way. Yes, you've launched a new clothing line, but was it impactful? Yes, you've released a new book, but was it impactful? Yes, you are productive, but are you impactful? Does your work produce favorable outcomes? Where are the results? Where are the receipts? Is the proof in the pudding?

Sometimes passion can have us caught up in the input that we don't consider our output. If you are intentional, you'll BE positively impactful. Remember that your ability determines what you're capable of doing. Your motivation determines what you do. Your attitude determines how well you do it. So, BE positively impactful in all that you do. Align your beliefs, words, and actions.

> **"You have a choice. Either you're going to whine or win. Either you're going to complain or contribute. You have to determine if you're going to complain or BE a catalyst of positive change."** -Anthony Broughton

Sometimes I feel like I should BE doing more to make a greater impact, but I've learned not to BE so hard on myself. There are so many people are who aren't producing anything. That's their business. Pat yourself on the back for at least being willing to bring about positive change. In fact, if you've formed a positive thought, that alone has a positive impact on you. You should pat yourself on the back for that as well. Don't seek recognition or validation for the work you're doing. Your true impact is incalculable. Let your impact speak for you! Our impact is not measured by what we say, it's measured by what we do.

Plant, Cultivate, Then Harvest

There are so many people that expect a harvest although they have not planted anything. Before you can reap, you must sow! You must then cultivate what you've sown. This is where BEing consistent comes back into play. You can sow all day, but if you are inconsistent with cultivating that seed it will not sprout. Even after the harvest, you must continue BEing consistent with planting and cultivating. In a nutshell, it takes consistent time and effort to truly make an impact. Don't focus on making a major impact, focus on making a meaningful impact! Yes, you planted 200 acres of dandelions, but what type of impact will it make? If you're going to sow into 200 acres of something,

BE intentional about what you sow, so that you can truly BE impactful. When you strive to BE a better you, you can no longer BE stuck on doing things just to do it. You have to BE intentional about where you channel your energy. So, if you truly want to BE impactful, you must learn to operate the gift within you. You have to overcome any doubt about who you are, what you can do, and what you can become, regardless of what others have to say. In fact, when you operate through your gift, you will impact the lives of those who hate and prey on you.

Solicit Feedback

So, you planted 200 acres of dandelions and you are so proud of the impact that you've made. You planted those dandelions because it was what you wanted to do. You didn't care about what others thought. However, you should care 'if' you are seeking to make a positive impact on others. It is essential to learn the values and needs of the population you intend to serve. Always conduct a needs-based assessment. Otherwise, you may have an adverse impact. Yes, you made an impact, but it was a meaningless impact. You want to always commit yourself to things that are worthwhile.

Considerations

My friend, Dr. Walter Lee, CEO of Impactful Enterprises, LLC says we should consider the following when BEing impactful:

- What population or groups of people will your product or service help?
- Do you use feedback as a means of improving yourself?
- How do you receive feedback? An attack? An opportunity?
    - When one is unsure of themselves, feedback can BE seen as a personal attack.
    - When one is confident about their vision, you see feedback as a pathway to self-improvement and sharpening your skill sets.
- Are you willing to create your own lane?

In the words of my mentor and fraternity brother, Don Weston, "It's ok to cross into other lanes if you need to get the job done. Do what you have to do! The work must get done!"

Just do the work! Don't seek recognition for the impact you are making. You will not always get a thank you note or a pat on the back for all you do. Just remember that God sees your work. You will always be disappointed if you strive to BE impactful to impress others. You can give your blood, sweat, and tears to making an impact and some people will still criticize you. So, just do the work. If you have haters hating on your work, at least you've impacted them by giving them something to hate on. Sometimes the people who have so much to say, aren't making an impact. **They're like an oak tree. They throw shade, but bear not fruit. Stay focused.**

-Anthony Broughton

CHAPTER 9

BE EXTRA-ORDINARY

BE EXTRA-ORDINARY

"All of us are seeking the same thing. We share the desire to fulfill the highest, truest expression of ourselves a human beings"

-Oprah Winfrey

"Either my skin tingles or my stomach churns. If my skin tingles, I know it's something I must do. If my stomach churns, I know it is something I cannot do."

-Cicely Tyson

Affirmation: I will overcome the fear of BEing who I am. I will overcome doubting if others will accept me.

What makes your skin tingle? What inspires you? What stirs you up? What makes you smile? What lights your fire? What excites you? What empowers you to move? What problem do you desire to solve? Whatever that something is can BE described as something you are passionate about. Passion is an energy. Operating in your extra-ness is one approach to fulfilling the highest expression of yourself. My mother always taught me to put my best foot forward. She is extremely passionate. She taught me to never half-do anything! She taught me to manifest my passion through my work! Give it your all! How people perceive it is their business! Give yourself permission to go above and beyond, regardless of how you may BE perceived. GO IN! You are on a mission! You have a purpose! Do not sit on any opportunity to manifest your passion. Tap into your passion and go all out with it—unapologetically. Do not dim your light because others chose not to let their light shine. Some people may BE envious and others may think you're "doing the most." That's their business—not yours. Don't choose to do the least when there's greater within you. When you operate within the greatness that has been invested in you, you will always BE extraordinary. It's a part of who you were made to BE and what you were called to do. Again, do your best and if others choose to do less, that's their business. Give them life!

You cannot control how and if someone decides to tap into their passion. In fact, we all have different passions. Not everyone knows what fuels you. Not everyone knows your calling. Not everyone knows your why! There will BE those who tell you that you're too extra, but they don't know your vision or your mission. You cannot focus on them or their mission. If you do, you'll lose sight on who you were called to BE. Some of us have spent our entire life making others happy and trying to satisfy others. We've all spent time trying to comply, assimilate, adapt to, and everything else, just to fit in and BE liked. However, there comes a time when you have to comply with your calling, assimilate to your aspirations, adapt to your anointing, and fit into your own shoes. There comes a time when you have to blaze your own trails. Time out for dehumanizing practices that force you to lose yourself to gain acceptance. Accept who you are and then if others choose to accept or deny you, that's on them. We weren't made for everyone to like or accept us. They should, but we should not expect them to.

You weren't created to BE liked, you were created to BE you.

Many people say I'm "extra." Blame my mother. I want to dedicate this portion of this chapter to my fellow "EXTRAS" who put the EXTRA in EXTRAordinary. When you fully embrace your extra-ness, you have to acknowledge that everyone cannot reciprocate extra-ness. They weren't built to BE extra. Some people go above and beyond at their capacity. Dr. T.D. Jakes talked about 10-gallon people. He cautioned us about expecting pint sized people to fulfill 10-gallon expectations. When we are operating in our extra-ness as 10-gallon people we have to BE mindful that everyone doesn't have the capacity to reciprocate the way we desire. They may BE reciprocating the best they can, within their capacity. They are BEing extra in their own unique way. This is why we must remember that we are unique. As such, we can't expect ourselves from other people. We set ourselves up for disappointment when we expect others to think, respond, and execute as we do. There is only one you. God really showed out making you.

Give Extra Love To #teamEXTRA

Many #teamEXTRA people are easily burned out. We pour our hearts and souls into everything we do. We go above and beyond and sometimes we feel that others don't reciprocate. Sometimes we feel unappreciated. Many people don't understand the behind the scenes effort that we put into what we do. It hurts at times. We feel drained. We feel empty, because no one pours into us after we've poured into others. #plottwist. That's our fault. We make a choice to pour our heart and soul into everything we do. We have the ability to choose how we radiate our energy. We choose what we focus on. We choose how much of ourselves we give to others. It's a choice. With that choice, we must also BE cautious not to over extend ourselves. Stop volunteering for everything and let others learn how to carry their weight. As extras, we must learn to BE Self-Caring (see Chapter 6). Rest and give others the opportunity to pull their weight.

Everyone and everything does not deserve you at your fullest capacity. Everyone doesn't deserve your extra-ness. Do not ever deplete yourself. Remain self-full. When you are empty you have nothing. When you are empty you have no choice but to seek something or someone to fill you up. Some of us call on God to fill us up, but God gave us common sense and wisdom. The bible verse says, "To whom much is given, much is required"—not ALL. All is not required, so take care of yourself.

Connect with other #teamextra people and they will give you life! Listen to an inspirational message on YouTube or a podcast from a person who inspires you. When I hear my mother speak or the words of Iyanla Vanzant, Oprah Winfrey, Dwuan Warmack, Matthew Stevenson, Cicely Tyson, Gloria Boutte, Adelaide Sanford, Mark Joseph, Christopher Emdin, Winston Holton, Jamila Lyiscott, Dywanna Smith, Roy Jones, Gloria Ladson Billings, Tabetha Brown, Queen Tribling, Julia Wright, T.D. Jakes, Tyler Perry and some others, it just moves me!

I also make time to connect with my #teamextra friends who give me life! Reciprocity is essential for those friends, because they share common struggles and moments of triumph. We must BE grateful for them, while also BEing accountable for holding them and ourselves accountable for unapologetically operating through our extra-ness, even when others think it's "too much." I always tell people that if I'm "too much," take that up with God. I have no control over how I was created.

It's Ok to BE Efficiently EXTRA

BE extraordinary and positively passionate about what you've been called to do. BE efficiently EXTRA. It is possible to BE extra in a negative and inefficient manner. Thus, if you're going to BE extra, BE efficient in what you do. Why settle for the status quo? Why do the bare minimum when you can give your best? My mantra has always been to do my best in all that I do. I believe that my work is a reflection of myself and those tied to me. I represent a legacy of excellence, so I'm going to produce excellence. You never know who will BE inspired or positively impacted by your work. Someone who did the bare minimum may BE inspired to BE more innovative because of your work. BE extraordinary, because the world needs your extra-ness! In a world that takes and takes and takes, a little extra will go a long way!

Don't Entertain Your Haters

Everyone isn't rooting for you! You may hear the noise and it may sound like cheers, but some people are cheering you on to fail! Your "haters" are truly disguised as lovers who have not yet developed the capacity and the skill set to truly communicate their love for you. They obviously love focusing on you. They obviously love speaking about you. There is something they love about you that they have not yet worked through. It is their issue—not yours. Don't feed them your attention. If you entertain a clown, you'll BE a part of the circus. Stay focused! The time you spend feeding your haters is the time you could BE feeding your potential. Let them hate while you BE great! Love them with the "church hug," even if they don't love you. STOP TRYING TO UNDERSTAND THE PURPOSE OF YOUR HATERS. Perhaps your haters are in your life to prevent you from being complacent. Perhaps if you didn't have haters, you wouldn't know that you possessed something worth capturing and maintaining the attention of others. Perhaps you have haters to not only inspire you but to compel you to BE who you were called to BE.

STOP TRYING TO UNDERSTAND YOUR HATERS! Your haters are oftentimes envious of the fact that you are making an impact and they aren't. They hate the fact that you are doing things they wish they could be doing. They hate you because they can't figure you out. They can't identify the ingredients in your formula of excellence. They question why they don't possess what you possess. The truth is, your excellence is encoded within your DNA and your mindset. You can't BE duplicated! You should also refrain from relinquishing time from your schedule and energy to entertain them. Remain aligned. Conserve your energy, but continue to root for them. Don't feed hate with hate. Feed hate with love, because love always win.

There is always a story or an underlying issue that undergirds why your haters are hating. It's coming from a place. It could BE a past experience or something traumatic that causes them to hate you for having what they don't have. You are not a counselor or a life coach. You are not responsible for helping them work through their trauma or issues. You are also not responsible for analyzing and helping them to unpack what causes them to hate you so much. You cannot control people. However, you can inspire them and love them from a distance. They may BE inspired and transformed by you choosing love over hate. The church folk would say, "Just pray for them." I'm telling you to pray for them with your ears and eyes open. Do this not out of fear, but to BE and remain vigilant and aligned at all times. However, if everyone is hating on you, you may need to engage in introspection. There may BE a misalignment in what you believe, say, and do.

BE Aligned

You don't want to ever BE extra in counterproductive or negative ways. We must remain aligned with our purpose to constantly operate within our gift with a sense of intentionality. When you operate within your gift, you are able to "fulfill the highest expression of yourself" (Oprah Winfrey). We are able to hone in on our most creative, artistic abilities, or the abilities of others to manifest our vision. Even with your extra-ness, you will not always BE able to execute your vision independently, because of the magnitude of your vision. We need to delegate and seek the support of other "extras."

Keep "Extra" People On Your Team

I'm not an event planner or decorator. I call on event planners and decorators who are extra. They will make you shine and help you manifest your vision more elaborately than you envisioned. Other "extra" people always blow my mind. We are easily burnt out, since we give so much as we channel our energy in extra-ordinary ways. Therefore, we have to BE supportive and commit ourselves to motivating, celebrating, and inspiring our fellow "extras" to continue to

BE efficiently extra. So, drop a compliment in their spirit, "Give the people life! Kill it! Go ham! Go beast mode! Serve the people! You better get it! Work! Ok, I see you! You did that," so they can continue to make the world a better place with their extraordinary ways. Hype them up!

BE Reflective

We must remain committed to reflection and co-flection if we truly want to make an impact. Even in our extra-ness, we must always BE reflective. We need to reflect on our impact. Are we happy with our work? How could we improve? Are there any opportunities for collaboration? Don't compete with other "extras". You should collaborate instead. Too much power (extra-ness) will blow a fuse!

The People Pleasing Poison

When are you getting married? When are you having children? When are you getting a house? When are you going back to school? When are you having another child? Where is your lover? When are you going to move? When are you going to apply for that position? When are you going to get a new house? Don't you think you need to _____?

I've lived most of my life trying to please others. I've tried to BE everything people wanted me to BE. There is so much painful, toxic pressure that comes with consuming people pleasing poison. Everyone has their idea of what happiness should look like for you. In fact, people can BE selfish by creating expectations for you to live up to. Sadly, people move the bar farther when you manage to reach the finish line of achieving their expectations. You've gotten married and had children as they wished and the question is now, "When are you having another child?" The expectations that people set for you can kill you if you normalize living your life BEing who others want you to BE. Your happiness is compromised for their happiness, as they live vicariously through you. Then you hit 40 and come to the realization that you spent the past 40 years living for others. You spent 40 years harboring EXTRAordinary talent, personality, insight, and value to fit in someone else's box. Don't do it!

People will have their positive or negative opinions of you regardless of what you do or what you say. You can become the first person to walk on Mars and people will say it's because you didn't fit in on Earth. Others will say, "You all are acting like he went to Saturn. It's *just* Mars." Some will say, "Look at how plain his spacesuit is." Your haters will probably say, "Oh, it took him 300 million miles just to get to Mars? It took me only 250 million." You'd think being the first to walk on Mars would be commendable, but it will never be good enough for haters.

Reverend Dr. Martin Luther King Jr. was awarded a whole, entire Nobel Peace Prize and people still said he was "the most dangerous man in America." People pleasing is one of the most dangerous habits to engage in. Snap out of it! Live your life for you! BE happy with who you are! There are married people with children who are miserable. There are people with children who disown or abuse them. There are people who have a mansion on top of the hill and still can't find happiness! There is no magic bullet to BEing happy. Live with no regrets. When people ask me questions about where is this and when will this happen, I remind them that things manifest when, how, and if

I *choose* to manifest them. Truthfully, people need to understand that some things are simply not their business. Some people ask about your love life when they can't keep a stable one. I've learned to appreciate the expectations of others, but I'm accountable for who I become and when I choose to BEcome. Either you love me for who I 'BE' or carry on and just let me BE. Either way, I will BE as the Great I AM has made me to BE. Some of the most bible bearing, religious practicing people won't make it to Heaven. If no sin is greater than the other, you can't pick and choose which sin you want to glorify over the others. We must work towards spirituality. Without a relationship with the creator, life is just a "show."

If you allow humans to set expectations for your life, you'll fail every time, because of human-error. No one on this Earth knows and sees all things. No one is perfect. As a result, no one is qualified to tell you how to live your life. Yes, we do want to value, listen, and learn from wise counsel on how to BE, but in the end when your BEing becomes WAS, you want to have no SHOULD'VES. You must BE courageous enough to acknowledge, confront and reject dehumanizing practices. BE you. Do you in such a way that your legacy will live on in spite of anyone or anything that tries to stop it. "And that's on Mary had a little lamb". BE EXTRAordinary in your own EXTRAordinary way!

Life is too short to do the bare minimum. You should maximize each moment. Do your best in all that you do. Go the extra mile. Be passionate! Be intentional! Put some effort in your work. Don't just exist. Live your life to the fullest. Don't be bland. Add season. Spice up your life! Spice of your work!

#BEEXTRA

-Anthony Broughton
"The Petty Professor"

CHAPTER 10

BE YOU

BE BETTER

"Your willingness to look at your darkness is what empowers you to change"
-Iyanla Vanzant

Affirmation: I will overcome the fear of BEing better. I will overcome doubting my potential.

M y prayer is always, "Use me, God. Show me how to take who I am, who I want to BE, and what I can do, and use it for a purpose greater than myself."

–Rev. Dr. Martin Luther King, Jr.

Don't get caught up in the gift. Concern yourself with the shift! There's a shift that must happen when you commit to unwrapping your gift. You must stir up your gift! Unleash your gift! Share your gift! Unapologetically, operate within your gift! Remember that God is using your situation to change you. We don't always see it initially, but we must continue to trust the process. We must remain vigilant to the various "teachable moments" of life. If we want to BE BETTER, we must work within, speak to, and call forth the better versions of ourselves to come forth, in spite of how difficult it may seem. We must speak against negativity and demolish all doubt.

The Danger of "What if?"

Consuming our minds with doubt limits us from BEing who we are called to BE. If we consume our time considering the "what ifs," we can miss out on opportunities to manifest the "what wills." What *will* you make happen?

But, what if they don't like me?

You were not created to BE liked. You were created to BE love and BE loved. So, BE love (give love) even when others don't give it. Forget the what ifs. Create the what will.

But, what if they don't like my work?

But, what if they adore your work? What if it's not about if they like your work, but rather if you produced your best work? There are people who haven't produced any work. At least you made the effort, when others didn't to produce something. Be proud of what you manifest. If they don't like it, that's their business. It's not a mandate for people to like everything. We all have different tastes. Your work will inspire those it is meant to inspire. Those who don't like your work, may be inspired to create something better. You would be the source of their inspiration.

But, what if they don't hire me?

But, what if they do hire you? What if there is a better opportunity for you? What if you don't have the master plan for your life? What if they selected a better candidate? What if your ego needs to be checked? What if you underestimated your potential? What if you have more preparation to do to prepare you for the position? What if they didn't hire you because God wanted to protect you from the unknown or reroute you to something greater? What if it's not what if they don't hire you, but rather when they hire you? What if you're supposed to be the person hiring you? What if you are suffering because you sat on your business idea?

But, what if I can't do the job?

But, what if you can do the job? You would not be in the position if you were incapable. If you are willing to learn and respect others, you will have the support you need to be successful. What if you remember that you don't know everything? It's ok to ask for help. However, it is equally important to BE prepared. Read all the information you can find related to your job. Research and speak with people who serve or have served in the position. What if you pursued every professional development opportunity to develop your skills? What if you remembered that "teamwork makes the dream work?" What if it's not what if you can't do the job, but rather *when* you do an awesome job?

But, what if they terminate me?

But, what if they are pleased with your work? What if your termination inspires you to work where you are valued and appreciated? What if your termination inspires you to work where you're able to operate within your gift? What if there are millions of other jobs and you do not have to settle or allow this one job to defeat you? What if you need to create your own job? What if there are lessons to be learned from a termination? What if you evolve as a result of a termination? What if it's not what if they terminate you, but rather when you terminate the old version of yourself? #reinventyourself

But, what if I fail at my goals?

But, what if you achieve your goals? What if you remember that you aren't perfect? What if you see your failure as a learning opportunity? What if you reflect upon your approach to reach your goals? What if you reapproached your goals more strategically, with more insight? What if your goals don't align with God's plan for your life? What if it's not what if you fail at your goals, but rather when you achieve your goals?

But, what if I get denied?

But, what if you get accepted? What if rejection is God's protection? What if a denial inspires you to be better? What if a denial reroutes you to something greater? What if a denial is an opportunity for self-reflection? What if a denial is caused by you applying for the wrong thing? What if it is not your time yet? What if it's not if you get denied, but rather *when* you get accepted?

But, what if I fail the test?

Reflect and Retake it, "by any means necessary." What if your failure inspires you to be better? What if you reapproach your preparation? What if your failure inspires you to seek support to develop your skills? What if it's not when you fail, but when you pass? You must invest in yourself and check your priorities.

But, what if my plan fails?

You are not the planner of your life. Try plan B-Z. What if you are executing the wrong plan? What if it's not when your plan fails, but when you succeed, regardless of the hurdles and obstacles that come your way.

But, what if they steal my ideas?

They can steal your recipe and it still taste like trash. There's more to it than the ingredients. You have to put your soul into it and that can't be duplicated. People can steal your ideas, but they can't steal your anointing. Your talents, gifts, and personality can't be duplicated.

But, what if they break my heart?

But, what if they are not allowed to break your heart? What if you guarded your heart? What if you don't give someone the power to break your heart?

Forget the what ifs! It's not what if, it's WHEN! Change your thoughts! Rephrase your statements when necessary to reflect your destiny. Speak positive words and affirmations into the atmosphere! Overcome doubt with your beliefs, words, and actions! You hold the power to BE who you were called to BEcome. You are a doubt demolisher! Demolish your doubts to WIN! BE you!

> Hate has 4 letters, so does Love
> Enemies has 7 letters, so does Friends
> Lying has 5 letters, so does truth
> Negative has 8, so does Positive
> Under has 5, so does Above
> Cry has 3 letters, so does Joy
> Anger has 5 letters, so does Happy
> Right has 5 letters, so does Wrong
> Hurt has 4 letters, so does Heal
> It means life is like a double-edged sword; so, transform
> every negative side into an aura of positivity.
> **We should choose the better side of the life.**
> -Author, unknown

The choice is yours.

BE _____

BE _____

BE _____

BE _____

BE _____

BE _____

BE _____

BE _____

BE _____

BE _____

BE A DOUBT DEMOLISHER

Words of Inspiration

"Simply live life. Enjoy it in real time. Meaning, embrace life in the moment. Learn and grow from every experience. Professionally and academically no obstacle is a barrier. You can overcome and achieve anything." -Travis Damon, *CEO of The Professional Gent*

"You have to go through a process before you can received the full package. The change I was praying for in my life came when I least expected it. That change you've been seeking is on the way. Don't give up yet." -Xavier L. Spann, *CEO of Right-Move Inspirations*

"Life is only truly lived if you're living for your passion. Understand your purpose and forget about what others think. Your path is your choice, but don't forget about your legacy." -Allen D. Taste, Jr., CEO of *The Educated Black Boy.*

"Continue to fight for what's yours even when others around you don't see it fit for you" - Jamarcus Little, *Author of Dreams Do Come True* available on Amazon

"To be successful is to breed a successor: who's next?" -TyKeith Mickens

"Before you get one win you have to take a thousand losses" -Nathaniel Bookman, Jr.

ABOUT THE AUTHOR

Dr. Anthony Broughton is an award-winning educator, Associate Professor of Education, Interim Department Chair, and Site Coordinator for the Call Me MISTER program at Claflin University. He is a native of Cross, South Carolina, who earned a Bachelor's of Science in Elementary Education from Benedict College, a Master's in Education from Columbia College, and a Doctor of Philosophy in Early Childhood Education from the University of South Carolina, by the age of 30. Dr. Broughton has served as a certified educator, regional pre-k coordinator at the SC Department of Education, adjunct instructor, and an administrator. Dr. Broughton is the chief consultant of Inspirational Voyages with MISTER, LLC. His educational consulting firm provides resources and culturally responsive professional development for teachers and administrators across the nation. He has presented and served as a keynote speaker at numerous conferences and events. Children around the world affectionately refer to Dr. Broughton as "MiSTER B," as they engage in his highly energetic and interactive educational videos, such as his hit song, "Watch the Letters Get Down," which has 1.6 million views (and counting) on YouTube. Dr. Broughton uses the name "MiSTER B" to pay homage to the "highly acclaimed" Call Me M.I.S.T.E.R. program, which played an instrumental role in his development as an educator and scholar. Dr. Broughton is an author and illustrator of four children's books and one academic book. Dr. Broughton serves on the national and state-level governing board member for the National Association for the Education of Young Children and served on the South Carolina Early Childhood Association board. He is a member of several organizations. He is a Life Member of Alpha Phi Alpha Fraternity, Incorporated, where he serves the community with his fraternity brothers. He has received several awards such as Claflin University Faculty of the Year 20-21, the inaugural SC Black Pages Top 40 under 40, The State Newspaper Top 20 under 40, the Call Me MISTER Trailblazer award, and the SCAEYC Lifetime Achievement Award-The Ralph Witherspoon Award, for his service to the community.

ADDITIONAL RESOURCES BY THE AUTHOR

Books

Music

**BOOK, FOLLOW, LIKE, SUBSCRIBE AND
CONNECT WITH THE AUTHOR AT**

www.misterbinpsires.com

 twitter
Dr.Anthony_MISTERB

 Instagram
MisterDrB

 Facebook
MisterDrB

Dr. Broughton provides keynotes, facilitates
numerous workshops, and conducts school visits.

Please leave a review for this book on Amazon!

Made in United States
Orlando, FL
29 April 2022